S0-BZR-419

ECUADOR

ESMERALDAS
TULCAN
QUITO
OCEANO PACIFICO
PORTOVIEJO
LATACUNGA
BABAHOYO
GUARANDA
AMBATO
GUAYAQUIL
RIOBAMBA
AZOGUES
MACHALA
CUENCA
LOJA

OLOMBIA
GALAPAGOS
PERU

Ediciones Delroisse agradecen a Su Excelencia Antonio José Lucio Paredes, Embajador del Ecuador en Francia, por la ayuda prestada a la presente obra.

Nous tenons à remercier son Excellence Monsieur Antonio José Lucio Paredes, Ambassadeur de l'Equateur auprès de la République Française pour l'aide apportée à la réalisation de ce livre.

We would like to thank His Excellency Mr. Antonio José Lucio Paredes, Ecuadorian Ambassador to the French Republic for his help in producing this book.

Wir danken hier besonders Seiner Exzellenz Antonio José Lucio Paredes, dem Gesandten Ecuadors in der französischen Republik, für seine wertvolle Mitarbeit, die in hohem Masse zur Fertigstellung dieses Buches beigetragen hat.

ECUADOR

Esta presentación intenta dar una visión panorámica, y por ende superficial, de un país enclavado en la mitad del mundo.

Sólo algunas palabras, luego hablarán las imágenes.

EQUATEUR

Le but de cette présentation est de donner une vision panoramique, et par conséquent superficielle, d'un pays enclavé au milieu du monde.

Rien que quelques mots, les images parleront ensuite.

ECUADOR

The purpose of this introduction is to give a panoramic, and therefore superficial, view of a country which is enclaved in the centre of the world.

Just a few words; the pictures will tell the rest of the story.

ECUADOR

Ziel dieser Beschreibung ist es, einen Gesamtüberblick - der natürlich nur oberflächlich sein kann - über ein Land, das inmitten der Welt eingekeilt ist, zu geben.

Nur einige Worte... die Bilder werden für sich selbst sprechen.

Datos geográficos

Situado al noroeste de Sudamérica, el Ecuador limita al norte con Colombia, al este y al sur con el Perú y al oeste con el océano Pacífico.

Posee tres regiones naturales ecológicamente diferenciadas entre sí: Costa, Sierra y Oriente. A mil kilómetros de sus costas están las islas Galápagos, que son una provincia del Ecuador.

Los Andes asientan sobre la geografía ecuatoriana dos cordilleras, la Oriental y la Occidental, que le dan al país una doble columna vertebral de hielo, lava y granito.

Costa

Feraces llanuras yacen entre la cordillera Occidental y el océano Pacífico. Setenta mil kilómetros cuadrados divididos en cinco provincias: Esmeraldas, Manabí, Guayas, Los Ríos y El Oro.

Bajo un clima cálido y húmedo, su tierra produce banano, café, cacao, caña de azúcar, arroz, variadas frutas y maderas abundantes, que se destinan principalmente al comercio externo.

El clima tropical de la Costa y los rayos verticales del sol son mitigados por la fría y bienhechora corriente de Humbolt. Existen dos épocas a lo largo del año, la una cálida y lluviosa llamada paradójicamente invierno (diciembre a mayo) y otra seca y menos cálida, conocida con el nombre de verano (junio a noviembre). La temperatura media oscila entre 26 y 29° C.

Los generosos sistemas fluviales del Guayas, el Esmeraldas y el Santiago riegan la tierra y sirven de vías de comunicación.

Guayaquil, puerto principal y polo de desarrollo industrial, es la ciudad más poblada del país, (alrededor de 850.000 habitantes).

Sierra

Las altas tierras ocupan 72.000 kilómetros cuadrados. El callejón interandino se interrumpe por nudos que forman hoyas y se conecta mediante la carretera Panamericana que es un triunfo del hombre sobre la geografía. Las provincias de la Sierra son: Carchi, Imbabura, Pichincha, Cotopaxi, Tungurahua, Bolívar, Chimborazo, Cañar, Azuay y Loja.

Volcanes y montañas son poemas telúricos de roca y nieve en la Sierra ecuatoriana. El Chimborazo alcanza 6.310 metros sobre el nivel del mar, el Cotopaxi sobrepasa los 6.000 metros y el Sangay (5.323 metros) es uno de los volcanes más activos del planeta.

El cultivo de la tierra, predominantemente practicado por la población indígeno-campesina, utiliza técnicas ancestrales y produce maíz, papas, cereales y, en general, mieses para el consumo interno. La modernización en el campo avanza cada día. La temperatura promedial es de 15° C.

Quito, capital de la República, a 2.800 metros sobre el nivel del mar, acomoda su traza urbana entre los pliegues del Pichincha, logrando una topografía acogedora y distinta. Centro político-administrativo del país, ha cobrado en el último lustro un considerable peso económico por el desarrollo de la industria petrolera y el crecimiento del sector público de la economía.

Otras ciudades de la zona interandina son: Cuenca, universitaria y cultural, que, por su población, es la tercera del país. Ambato, Riobamba, Loja, Ibarra y muchas otras ciudades menores, ejemplifican un proceso de crecimiento urbano en detrimento del área rural.

Oriente

Raudales de futuro para el país; vegetación exuberante, clima tropical amazónico, variada fauna, zona poco poblada que carece aún de una infraestructura suficiente para un desarrollo sostenido de su potencial económico. El Oriente es el habitat de grupos silvícolas tales como los Cofanes, los Sionas, los Secoyas, los Záparos, los Canelos, los Yumbos, los Aucas, los Shuaras, los Jívaros y otros asentamientos humanos de estructura social simple.

La región nor-oriental genera actualmente más de 200.000 barriles de petróleo, que ubican a nuestro país como el segundo exportador latinoamericano de hidrocarburos.

Las provincias de Napo, Pastaza, Morona-Santiago y Zamora-Chinchipe son realidad y promesa, posibilidad y desafío.

Galápagos

A mil kilómetros de nuestras costas se encuentra el archipiélago de Colón o islas Galápagos, su nombre viene de las tortugas gigantes o "galápagos" (geochelone elephantopus).

Maravilloso laboratorio natural, Galápagos, con su rostro de granito y lava, alberga especies de fauna únicas en el mundo. Durante el siglo XVII es guarida de piratas y corsarios. En 1853 Charles Darwin estudia las especies vivas de las islas y formula su teoría de la evolución, que va a conmocionar el mundo científico de la época. La adaptación al medio y la selección natural son hipótesis que provocan apasionados duelos académicos en aquel entonces.

Actualmente el Gobierno ecuatoriano, para proteger las islas, las ha declarado Parque Nacional. En la isla Santa Cruz funciona la estación "Charles Darwin" que proteje este patrimonio de la ciencia universal.

Galápagos es un extraño mundo que emerge del pasado y advierte al hombre, mamifero depredador, sobre la necesidad de un justo equilibrio ecológico.

Población

Según el censo de 1974, y considerando un crecimiento demográfico del 3,4% anual, el Ecuador tiene alrededor de siete millones y medio de habitantes, con una densidad poblacional media de 22 habitantes por kilómetro cuadrado

El proceso histórico ha producido un mestizaje generalizado que obliga a utilizar criterios socio-culturales para estudiar los grupos étnicos. En la Costa deja sentir su presencia el montuvio, con excepción de la provincia de Esmeraldas donde abunda la población negra.

En la Sierra, predomina el campesino-indígena que, sometido al proceso de migración rural-urbana, se vuelve cada vez más «mestizo».

Las minorías etno-culturales, como los Cayapas, los Colorados (grupo en avanzado estado de aculturación) y los grupos selváticos del Oriente, ven en peligro su supervivencia, y el de sus rasgos culturales específicos, ante el avance de la sociedad técnica.

Una demografía desarmónica, concentración en ciertas zonas y baja densidad poblacional en otras, caracteriza al espacio nacional ecuatoriano.

UNA MIRADA AL PASADO

Estudios sistemáticos en el campo de la Antropología, permiten afirmar que el Ecuador posee por los menos 12.000 años de cultura. Esto no significa que no existan vestigios más antiguos, sino que desde hace 12.000 años tenemos documentos arqueológicos coherentes sobre el período *Precerámico*, que se extiende entre le décimo y el cuarto milenario antes de nuestra Era. Esta época está caracterizada por un seminomadismo de grupos humanos predatores, es decir, que vivían principalmente de la cacería y la recolección de frutos silvestres. El sitio El Inga en los alrededores de Quito, es el más representativo de este período conocido también con el nombre de Paleoindio.

3.200 años antes de nuestra Era, se inicia el período *Formativo,* caracterizado por el hecho de que el hombre comienza a sembrar la tierra, lo cual conduce a un grado de sedentarización mayor. Dentro de este período la fase Valdivia se destaca como la primera cultura cerámica del nuevo mundo. Son notables las figuras antropomorfas, conocidas como «venus» de Valdivia.

Las fases Machalilla y Chorrera, pertenecen también al Formativo. En la cultura Chorrera aparecen las vasijas-silbato que son recipientes de cerámica que emiten sonidos musicales cuando el aire es desplazado por el líquido contenido en el recipiente.

500 años antes de nuestra Era comienza un nuevo periodo llamado *Desarrollo regional,* que va a durar hasta el siglo V de nuestra Era. En estos mil años se destacan las fases de Guangala, Bahía, Jama-Coaque, la Tolita, Narrio II, Panzaleo I y Tuncahuán.

El hombre muestra su alto sentido estético en las piezas de cerámica y en el trabajo de los metales. Para no citar sino un ejemplo, en la fase La Tolita se trabajó el platino hace dos mil quinientos años, mientras en Europa dicho metal comienza apenas a laborarse en el siglo XVIII.

Entre el siglo V y el siglo XV de nuestra Era se desenvuelve el período de *Integración,* dentro del cual sobresalen las fases Milagro-Quevedo, Manteño, Jama-Coaque II, Tacalshapa, Cashaloma, Panzaleo II y III, Puruhá, Negativo-del-Carchi y Cuasmal.

Adviene entonces el período de resistencia a la *Dominación incaica,* que dura únicamente alrededor de sesenta anos y se ejerce sobre todo en la Sierra ecuatoriana. En la provincia des Canar queda como testimonio Ingapirca, un templo al sol que es la obra arquitectónica mayor del Incario en nuestras tierras. Quito se convierte en la segunda capital del Tahuantinsuyo. Es un error considerar a todo nuestro pasado como incaico ya que, como vemos, este período es muy corto en el tiempo. Los Cronistas de Indias difunden este error que, por desgracia, subsiste con frecuencia.

El siglo XVI está marcado históricamente por el descubrimiento, la conquista y la colonización de América por Europa. El período colonial produce el mestizaje étnico y cultural que hoy caracteriza al Ecuador. La Colonia, con las profundas injusticias sociales de la época, genera un arte escultórico y pictórico conocido justamente con el nombre de Arte Colonial.

El 10 de agosto de 1809 en Quito se lanza el primer grito de la independencia americana. El 24 de mayo de 1822, luego de la batalla del Pichincha, en la que combate Antonio José de Sucre, lugarteniente del libertador Simón Bolivar, el país es anexado a la Gran Colombia. En 1830 comienza la época republicana.

A partir de 1972 el Ecuador, de país agro-exportador, se convierte en agro-minero-exportador. Es la presencia del petróleo la que va a modificar sus relaciones sociales de producción y por ende el curso de su historia. El Nuevo Mundo será un día un mundo nuevo.

ECUADOR
12.000 Años de Cultura

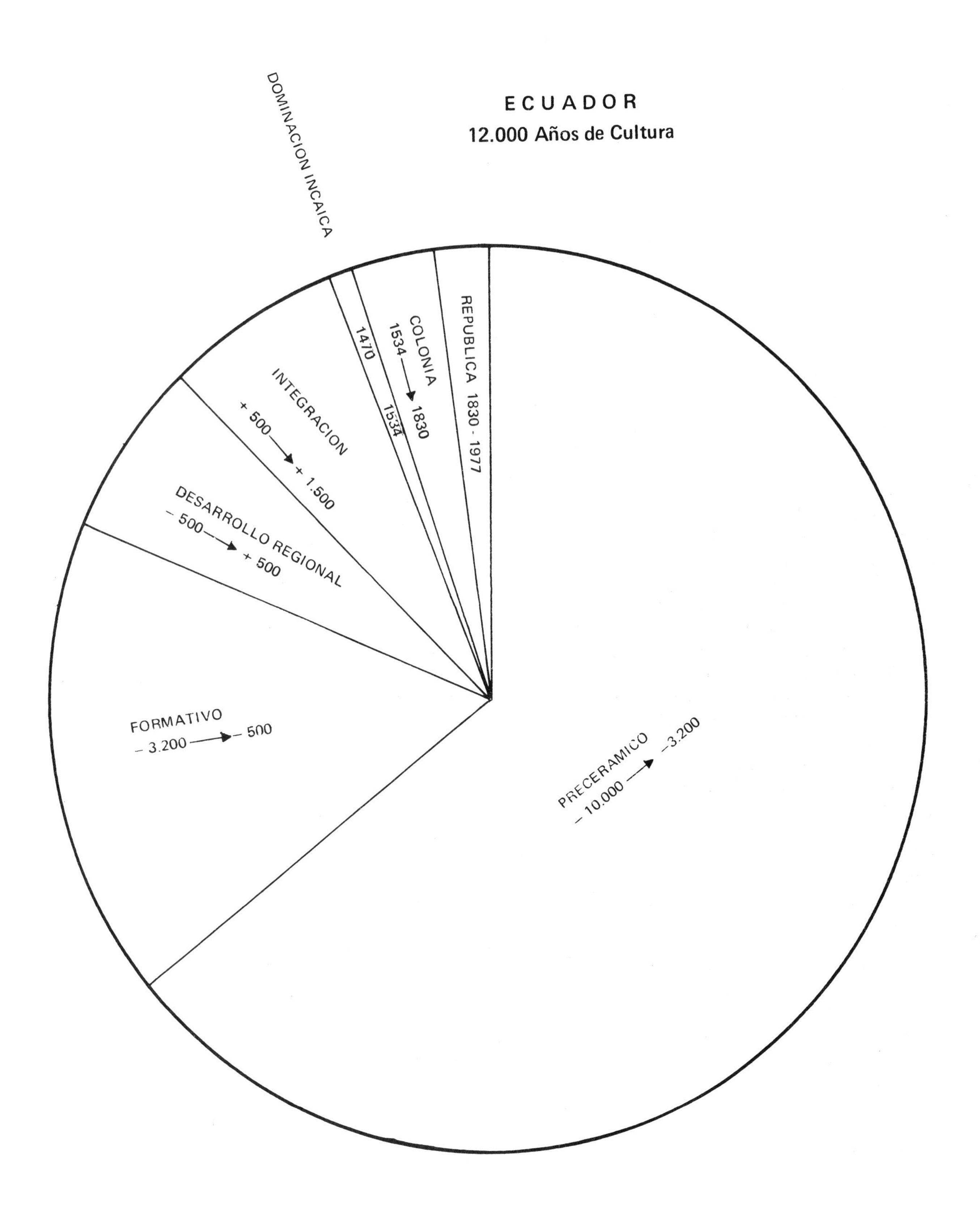

ASPECTOS ECONOMICOS

La economía ecuatoriana está sustentada básicamente por el llamado sector primario. El cultivo de la tierra es el rubro de actividad dominante; cabe dividirlo en agricultura de exportación y agricultura para el mercado interno.

Los principales productos agrarios de exportación son: banano, café y cacao.

La economía de nuestro pais depende en muy alto grado del comercio exterior. El apogeo de la llamada época del cacao se sitúa entre 1880 y 1920. El banano logra su punto más alto en la década de 1950 a 1960.

La agricultura, la silvicultura y la pesca contribuyen al producto nacional bruto con un 40% aproximadamente. La manufactura representa un 16%. El producto nacional bruto en 1972 fue de 1.776 millones de U.S. dólares y pasó a 4.204 millones de U.S. dólares en 1975.

La principales industrias son la alimenticia y la textil. Existen además la de productos quimicos y medicinas, la de pulpa y papel, la siderúrgica, la micromecánica, la electrónica, la metal-mecánica, la de cemento, de azúcar, de tabaco, entre otras actividades fabriles. El ingreso anual per-cápita es de ± 600 U.S. dólares.

Toda la industria petrolera, incluida la refinería estatal de Esmeraldas, constituye un hecho nuevo en la economía nacional; efectivamente, una producción de 210.000 barriles diarios de petróleo, es transportada por el oleoducto transecuatoriano que, partiendo de Lago Agrio en el Oriente, llega al puerto petrolero de Balao en Esmeraldas. La Corporación Estatal Petrolera Ecuatoriana —CEPE— posee el 62,5% de las acciones del consorcio petrolero Texaco-Cepe. En su calidad de exportador neto de petróleo el Ecuador forma parte de la Organización de Países Exportadores de Petróleo —OPEP—. El país recibe cerca de 12 dólares por cada barril de petróleo que exporta.

La tasa de rentabilidad de las empresas que trabajan en el Ecuador es altamente positiva. En un afán de integración económica y expansión de mercados, nuestro país forma parte del llamado Pacto Andino, conjuntamente con Venezuela, Colombia, Perú y Bolivia.

La riqueza ictiológica, las reservas madereras y el subsuelo minero constituyen un interesante potencial para un desarrollo intenso y sobre todo armónico de la economía nacional.

Los extraordinarios atractivos turísticos del Ecuador se expresan por sí solos en las fotografías de la presente obra.

La estabilidad monetaria completa este ligero panorama de la economía ecuatoriana.

ASPECTOS CULTURALES

El patrimonio cultural ecuatoriano se destaca por su originalidad y riqueza. La simbiosis de la cultura greco-latina-europea con las raíces culturales aborígenes, produjo un barroco andino que se plasma en iglesias y conventos que, a justo título, están consideradas como las mejores del continente. San Francisco, —siglo XVI— y la Compania —siglo XVII— son ejemplos elocuentes. La llamada «Escuela Quiteña» produjo artistas como Pampite, Legarda, Caspicara, Miguel de Santiago, Goríbar, Sangurima, para no citar sino a las figuras descollantes.

La tradición plástica se mantiene vigente. En pintura, por ejemplo, tenemos creadores tan destacados como Oswaldo Guayasamín, Manuel Rendón Seminario, Eduardo Kingman, Enrique Tábara, Oswaldo Viteri, Luis Molinari, Estuardo Maldonado, Aníbal Villacis, entre muchos otros artífices de un arte vario y fecundo, que ocupa un destacado sitial dentro de la plástica latinoamericana contemporánea.

En el campo de las Letras, cuya tradición viene desde el indio Espejo en la colonia, el llamado «Grupo de Guayaquil» con Gallegos Lara, De La Cuadra, Pareja Diezcanseco, Aguilera Malta y Gil Gilbert, tienen su puesto en las letras continentales.

Citemos solamente a Angel Felicísimo Rojas y Jorge Icaza, como novelistas; César Dávila Antrade, Gonzalo Escudero, Jorge Carrera Andrade y Jorge Enrique Adoum como poetas.

Benjamín Carrión es el gran propulsor del quehacer literario actual.

Inquietudes interesantes se dejan ver en el campo de la investigación social. Actividades como el teatro, la danza, la música y el cine nacional tienen aún un largo camino por andar.

Juan CUEVA Jaramillo
París, febrero de 1977.

EQUATEUR

DONNEES GEOGRAPHIQUES

Situé au Nord-Ouest de l'Amérique du Sud, l'Equateur est délimité au Nord par la Colombie, à l'Est et au Sud par le Pérou et à l'Ouest par l'Océan Pacifique.

Il possède trois régions naturelles écologiquement différenciées entre elles: la Costa, la Sierra, et l'Oriente. A mille kilomètres de ses côtes se situent les îles Galapagos, qui sont une province de l'Equateur.

La géographie équatorienne est marquée par le développement des Andes en deux cordillères, l'Orientale et l'Occidentale, qui donnent au pays une double colonne vertébrale de glace, de lave et de granit.

Costa. Des plaines fertiles s'étendent entre la cordillère occidentale et l'Océan Pacifique. Soixante dix mille kilomètres carrés divisés en cinq provinces : Esmeraldas, Manabi, Guayas, Los Rios et El Oro.

Sous un climat chaud et humide, sa terre produit des bananes, du café, du cacao, de la canne à sucre, du riz, une gamme très étendue de fruits et des bois abondants destinés principalement au commerce extérieur.

Le climat tropical de la Costa et les rayons verticaux du soleil sont atténués par le froid et bienfaisant courant de Humboldt. Il existe deux époques dans l'année, l'une chaude et pluvieuse appelée paradoxalement hiver (de décembre à mai) et l'autre sèche et moins chaude, connue sous le nom d'été (de juin à novembre). La température moyenne oscille entre 26 et 29° C.

Les généreux systèmes fluviaux du Guayas, de l'Esmeraldas et du fleuve Santiago irriguent les terres et servent de voies de communication.

Guayaquil, port principal et pôle de développement industriel, est la ville la plus peuplée du pays (environ 850.000 habitants).

Sierra. Les hautes terres couvrent une surface de 72.000 kilomètres carrés. Le couloir interandin présente une succession de hauts bassins séparés par des seuils et reliés par la route Panaméricaine qui est un triomphe de l'homme sur la nature. Les provinces de la Sierra sont : Carchi, Imbabura, Pichincha, Cotopaxi, Tungurahua, Bolivar, Chimborazo, Cañar, Azuay et Loja.

Sierra. Les hautes terres couvrent une surface de 72.000 kilomètres carrés. Le couloir interandin présente une succession de hauts bassins séparés par des seuils et reliés par la route Panaméricaine qui est un triomphe de l'homme sur la nature. Les provinces de la Sierra sont : Carchi, Imbabura, Pichincha, Cotopaxi, Tungurahua, Bolivar, Chimborazo, Cañar, Azuay et Loja.

Volcans et montagnes sont de véritables symphonies telluriques de roche et de neige dans la Sierra équatorienne. Le Chimborazo atteint 6.310 mètres au-dessus du niveau de la mer, le Cotopaxi dépasse les 6.000 mètres et le Sangay (5.323 mètres) est l'un des volcans les plus actifs de la planète.

L'agriculture pratiquée presque exclusivement par une population de paysans indigènes, utilise des techniques ancestrales et produit du maïs, des pommes de terre, des céréales et, en général, les récoltes de la consommation intérieure. La modernisation rurale progresse chaque jour. La température moyenne est de 15° C.

Quito, capitale de la République, à 2.800 mètres au-dessus du niveau de la mer, aménage son plan urbain entre les plis du Pichincha, présentant ainsi une topographie accueillante et inhabituelle. Centre politique et administratif du pays, elle a acquis depuis cinq ans un considérable poids économique grâce au développement de l'industrie pétrolière et à l'accroissement du secteur public de l'économie.

Les autres villes de la zone interandine sont : Cuenca, ville universitaire et culturelle qui, par sa population, est la troisième du pays. Ambato, Riobamba, Loja, Ibarra et bien d'autres encore, mais moins importantes, sont l'exemple même du processus d'accroissement urbain au détriment de l'aire rurale.

Oriente. Région riche en promesses pour l'avenir du pays; végétation exubérante, climat tropical amazonien, faune variée, zone peu peuplée qui manque encore d'une infrastructure suffisante pour un développement soutenu de son potentiel économique. La population de l'Oriente est constituée de groupes sylvicoles comme les Cofanes, les Sionas, les Secoyas, les Záparos, les Canelos, les Yumbos, les Aucas, les Shuaras, les Jivaros et autres groupes humains de structure sociale simple.

La région nord-orientale produit actuellement plus de 200.000 barils de pétrole, ce qui fait de notre pays le deuxième exportateur latino-américain d'hydrocarbures.

Les provinces de Napo, Pastaza, Morona-Santiago et Zamora-Chinchipe sont réalité et promesse, possibilité et défi.

Galápagos. A mille kilomètres de nos côtes, se trouve l'archipel Colón ou îles Galápagos; son nom lui vient des tortues géantes ou "galápagos" (geochelone elephantopus).

Merveilleux laboratoire naturel, les Galápagos, avec leur visage de granit et de lave, abritent des espèces d'une faune unique au monde. Durant le XVIIème siècle ces îles servirent de repaire de pirates et de corsaires. En 1853 Charles Darwin étudie les espèces vivantes des îles et formule sa théorie sur l'évolution des espèces qui va bouleverser le monde scientifique de l'époque. L'adaptation au milieu et la sélection naturelle sont des hypothèses qui provoquèrent des duels académiques passionnés en ce temps-là.

Actuellement le Gouvernement Equatorien, afin de protéger ces îles, les a déclarées Parc National. Dans l'île Santa Cruz le centre "Charles Darwin" protège ce patrimoine de science universelle.

Les Galápagos, ce monde étrange qui émerge du passé, met en garde l'homme, ce mammifère déprédateur, sur la nécessité d'un juste équilibre écologique.

Population. D'après le recensement de 1974, et tenant compte d'un accroissement démographique de 3,4% annuel, l'Equateur a environ sept millions et demi d'habitants, avec une densité de 22 habitants par kilomètre carré.

Le processus historique a produit un métissage généralisé qui oblige à se référer à de véritables critères socio-culturels pour étudier les groupes ethniques. La Côte est le domaine du paysan "montuvio", à l'exception toutefois de la province d'Esmeraldas qui a une population à prédominance noire.

Dans les Andes, prédomine le paysan indigène, soumis au processus des migrations vers les villes et de plus en plus "métissé".

La progression de la société technique menace la survie de minorités ethnoculturelles, comme les Cayapas, les Colorados (en état avancé d'acculturation) et autres groupes selvatiques de l'Oriente, et partant celle de leurs traits culturels spécifiques.

Une séparation démographique très inégale, concentration dans certaines zones et faibles densités de population dans d'autres, caractérisent l'espace national équatorien.

COUP D'OEIL SUR LE PASSE

Des études systématiques dans le domaine de l'Anthropologie permettent d'affirmer que l'Equateur possède au moins 12.000 ans de culture. Ce qui ne signifie pas qu'il n'y ait de vestiges plus anciens, mais que depuis 12.000 ans nous possédons des documents archéologiques cohérents sur la période PRECERAMIQUE, qui s'étend entre le dixième et le quatrième millénaire avant notre Ere. Cette époque est caractérisée par un semi-nomadisme de groupes humains prédateurs, c'est-à-dire, qui vivaient principalement de la chasse et de la cueillette des fruits. Le site El Inga aux alentours de Quito, est le plus représentatif de cette période connue aussi sous le nom de Paléoindienne.

3.200 ans avant notre Ere, débute la période primaire, caractérisée par le fait que l'homme commence à cultiver la terre, ce qui le conduit à un degré de sédentarisation plus grand. A l'intérieur de cette période la phase Valdivia se détache comme la première culture céramique du nouveau monde. Il convient de mentionner les figures anthropomorphes, connues comme "vénus" de Valdivia.

Les phases Machalilla et Chorrera, appartiennent aussi à la période PRIMAIRE. Dans la culture Chorrera apparaissent les bouteilles-sifflets qui sont des récipients de céramique qui émettent des sons musicaux lorsque l'air est déplacé par le liquide contenu dans le récipient.

500 ans avant notre ère débute une nouvelle période appelée DEVELOPPEMENT REGIONAL, qui va durer jusqu'au Vème siècle de notre Ere. Dans ces mille années se détachent les phases de Guangala, Bahià, Jama-Coaque, la Tolita, Narrio II, Panzaleo I et Tuncahuán.

L'homme montre son haut sens esthétique dans les pièces de céramique et dans le travail des métaux. Pour ne citer qu'un exemple, dans la phase La Tolita on travaillait déjà le platine il y a deux mille cinq cents ans, alors qu'en Europe il faudra attendre le dix-huitième siècle.

Entre le Vème et le XVème siècle de notre Ere se situe la période d'INTEGRATION, à l'intérieur de laquelle se détachent les phases culturelles Milagro-Quevedo, Manteño, Jama-Coaque II, Tacalshapa, Cashaloma, Panzaleo II et III, Puruhá, Negativo-del-Carchi et Cuasmal.

On assiste alors à la période de résistance à la DOMINATION INCA qui durera quelques soixante ans et s'exercera surtout dans la Sierra équatorienne. Dans la province de Cañar à Ingapirca, un temple du soleil témoigne de cette période; c'est l'œuvre architecturale la plus importante laissée par les Incas sur nos terres. Quito devient la seconde capitale du Tahuantinsuyo. Ce serait une erreur de considérer tout notre passé comme inca puisque, comme nous le voyons, il ne s'agit là que d'un moment très court dans le temps. Les Chroniqueurs des Indes répandent cette erreur qui, malheureusement, subsiste.

Le XVIème siècle est marqué historiquement par la découverte, la conquête et la colonisation de l'Amérique par l'Europe (L'Espagne joue un rôle fondamental). La période coloniale produit le métissage ethnique et culturel qui aujourd'hui caractérise l'Equateur. La Colonie, malgré les profondes injustices sociales de l'époque, engendre un art sculptural et pictural connu précisément sous le nom d'Art Colonial. En 1542, Francisco de Orellana découvre le fleuve Amazone à la tête d'une expédition organisée et financée depuis Quito.

Le 10 août 1809 retentit sur Quito le premier cri d'Indépendance américaine. Le 24 mai 1822, après la bataille de Pichincha, à laquelle prend part Antonio José de Sucre, lieutenant du libérateur Simon Bolivar, le pays s'annexe à la Gran Colombia. En 1830 commence l'époque républicaine.

A partir de 1972 l'Equateur passe du stade d'exportateur agricole au stade d'exportateur-agricole-et-minier. C'est la présence du pétrole qui va modifier ses relations sociales de production et par là-même le cours de son histoire. Le Nouveau Monde sera un jour un monde nouveau.

ASPECTS ECONOMIQUES

Fondamentalement, l'économie équatorienne repose sur le secteur primaire. L'agriculture est l'activité dominante; il convient de la diviser en agriculture d'exportation et agriculture pour le marché intérieur.

Les principaux produits agricoles d'exportation sont : la banane, le café et le cacao.

L'économie de notre pays dépend en grande partie du commerce extérieur. L'apogée de ce que l'on peut appeler l'époque du cacao se situe entre 1880 et 1920. La banane atteint son point le plus haut dans la décade de 1950 à 1960.

L'agriculture, la sylviculture et la pêche contribuent pour environ 40% au produit national brut, les produits manufacturés interviennent pour 16%. Le produit national brut en 1972 fut de 1.776 millions de dollars U.S. et atteint 4.204 millions de cette monnaie en 1975. Les principales industries sont l'industrie alimentaire et l'industrie textile; il existe en plus celle des produits chimiques et des médicaments, celle de la pâte à papier et du papier lui-même, la sidérurgie, la mécanique de précision, l'électronique, l'industrie du métal, celle du ciment, du sucre, du tabac, entre autres activités manufacturières. Le revenu annuel par tête est de ± 600 U.S. dollars en Equateur.

Toute l'industrie pétrolière, y compris la raffinerie d'état d'Esmeraldas, constitue un fait nouveau dans l'économie nationale; en effet, tous les jours une production de 210.000 barils de pétrole est transportée par l'oléoduc transéquatorien qui, partant de Lago Agrio dans la province de l'Oriente, arrive au port pétrolier de Balao dans la province d'Esmeraldas. La "Corporación Estatal Petrolera Ecuatoriana" -CEPE-, possède 62,5% des actions du consortium pétrolier Texaco-Cepe. En sa qualité d'exportateur net de pétrole l'Equateur fait partie de l'Organisation des Pays Exportateurs de Pétrole -OPEP-. Le pays reçoit près de 12 dollars par baril de pétrole qu'il exporte.

Le taux de rentabilité des entreprises qui travaillent en Equateur est très nettement positif. Dans un désir d'intégration économique et d'expansion des marchés, notre pays fait partie du célèbre Pacte Andin, conjointement avec le Vénézuéla, la Colombie, le Pérou et la Bolivie.

La richesse ichtyologique, les réserves de bois et le sous-sol minier, constituent un intéressant potentiel pour un développement intense et harmonique de l'économie nationale.

Les extraordinaires attraits touristiques de l'Equateur parlent d'eux-mêmes, ainsi qu'en témoignent les photos de cet ouvrage.

La stabilité monétaire complète ce rapide panorama de l'économie équatorienne.

ASPECTS CULTURELS

Le patrimoine culturel équatorien se distingue par son originalité et sa richesse. La symbiose de la culture greco-latino-européenne avec les racines culturelles aborigènes, produisit un barroque andin qui se concrétise dans des églises et des couvents qui, à juste titre, sont considérés comme les meilleurs du continent. San Francisco -XVIème siècle- et la Compañia -XVIIème siècle- sont des exemples éloquents. La célèbre "Escuela Quiteña" produisit des artistes comme Pampite, Legarda, Caspicara, Miguel de Santiago, Goribar, Sangurima, pour ne citer que les figures les plus marquantes.

La tradition plastique est toujours en vigueur. En peinture, par exemple, nous avons des créateurs aussi remarquables que Oswaldo Guayasamín, Manuel Rendón Semanario, Eduardo Kingman, Enrique Tábara, Oswaldo Viteri, Luis Molinari, Estuardo Maldonado, Aníbal Villacís, entre autres auteurs d'un art varié et fécond, qui occupe une place de choix à l'intérieur de la plastique latino-américaine contemporaine.

Dans le domaine des Lettres, dont la tradition remonte à l'indien Espejo au temps de la colonie, le fameux "Grupo de Guayaquil", avec Gallegos Lara, De La Cuadra, Pareja Diezcanseco, Aguilera Malta et Gil Gilbert, tient sa place dans les lettres continentales.

Citons seulement Angel Felicísimo Rojas et Jorge Icaza, comme romanciers; César Dávila Andrade, Gonzalo Escudero, Jorge Carrera Andrade et Jorge Enrique Adoum comme poètes.

Benjamin Carrión est le grand propulseur du travail littéraire actuel.

On note des inquiétudes intéressantes dans le domaine de la recherche sociale. Des activités comme le théâtre, la danse, la musique et le cinéma national ont encore un long chemin à parcourir.

Juan CUEVA Jaramillo

GEOGRAPHY

Ecuador, in the North-West of South America, is surrounded by Colombia to the North, Peru to the East and South and the Pacific Ocean to the West.

Ecuador has three distinct zones each with a specific ecology - Costa, Sierra and Oriente. A thousand kilometres from the mainland are the Galapagos Islands, which constitute a province of Ecuador. The geography of Ecuador is characterized by the division of the Andes into two cordilleras, forming a double vertebral column of ice, lava and granite.

Costa. Fertile plains spread out between the Western Cordillera and the Pacific Ocean. These cover 70,000 square kilometres divided into five provinces - Esmeraldas, Manabi, Guayas, Los Rios and El Oro. With a hot, moist climate, the soil produces bananas, coffee, cocoa, cane sugar, rice, a very wide range of fruit and abundant wood, most of which is exported.

The tropical climate of Costa and the vertical rays of the sun are attenuated by the beneficial cooling effect of Humboldt's currents. There are two seasons in the year - one hot and rainy known paradoxically as winter, and the other dry and less hot known as summer; they last from December to May and from June to November respectively.

Average temperature varies between 26 and 29°C.

The river systems of the Guayas, the Esmeraldas and the Santiago irrigate the soil and are used as a means of communication.

Guayaquil, the chief port and a centre of industrial development, is the town with the largest population (about 850.000).

Sierra. The Highlands cover an area of 72,000 square kilometres. The space between the two mountain ranges of the Andes consists of a series of lofty basins separated by sills and connected up by the Pan-American Highway, which is a triumph of man over nature. The provinces of the Sierra are Carchi, Imbabura, Pichincha, Cotopaxi, Tungurahua, Bolivar, Chimborazo, Cañar, Azuay and Loja.

Volcanoes and mountains are absolute earthly symphonies of rock and snow in the Ecuadorian Sierra. The Chimborazo rises to 6,310 metres (about 21,000 feet) above sea level, the Cotopaxi is over 6,000 metres (20,000 feet), and the Sangay (5,323 metres or about 18,000 feet) is one of the most active volcanoes in the world.

Farming, which is carried on almost exclusively by a population of native farmers, is based on ancestral methods and produces maize, potatoes, cereals and, generally speaking, crops for domestic consumption. Farming methods are now being constantly modernised. The average temperature is 15°C.

Quito, the capital of the Republic, at 2,800 metres (9,300 feet) above sea level, is laid out between the folds of the Pichincha, which gives it an unusual topography, though a hospitable one. It is the political and administrative centre of the country and, over the past five years, has achieved considerable economic importance owing to the development of the petroleum industry and the growth of the public sector of the economy.

The other towns of the Inter-Andean Zone are Cuenca - a university town and cultural centre which has the third largest population in the country - Ambato, Riobamba, Loja, Ibarra and many others which, though smaller, provide an illustration of the increase in the size of towns at the expense of the country.

Oriente. This region constitutes a promise for the future of the country, with its exuberant vegetation, its Amazonian tropical climate, its wide variety of fauna and its sparse population, which still lacks the infrastructure necessary for the sustained development of its economic potential. The population of Oriente consists of forest-dwelling tribes such as the Cofanes, Sionas, Secoyas, Zaparos, Canelos, Yumbos, Aucas, Shuaras, Jivaros and other tribus with a primitive social structure.

The North of the Oriente Region is at present producing more than 200,000 barrels of petroleum a day, with the result that Ecuador is the second Latin-American exporter of hydro-carbides.

The provinces of Napo, Pastaza, Morona-Santiago and Zamora-Chinchipe are reality and promise, possibility and a challenge.

Galapagos. A thousand kilometres from the mainland lies the Colon Archipelago or Galapagos Islands; the name is derived from that of the giant tortoises (geochelone elephantopus) which are found there.

The Galapagos Islands, with their landscape of granite and lava, constitute an absolute natural history museum, for they contain species of fauna which are not found anywhere else in the world. During the seventeenth century these islands were used as a refuge by pirates and filibusters. In 1853 Charles Darwin made a study of the species living in the islands and worked out his theory of evolution of the species, which revolutionized the scientific world of that time. His theories of adaptation to the environment and natural selection gave rise to passionate academic duels among his contemporaries.

The Government of Ecuador has now declared these islands a national park, with the aim of protecting them. The "Charles Darwin" Centre on the island of Santa Cruz is responsible for the protection of this universal science heritage.

The strange world of the Galapagos Islands, emerging out of the distant past, is a warning to Man, that destructive mammal, regarding the necessity for a proper ecological balance.

Population. According to the 1974 census, and assuming an annual population increase of 3.4%, Ecuador has about seven and a half million inhabitants, with a density of 22 inhabitants per square kilometre.

History has resulted in widespread interbreeding, which makes it necessary to refer to real socio-cultural criteria in order to study the ethnic groups. The montuvio peasant is predominant on the coast, though with the exception of the Province of Esmeraldas, where the population is predominantly black.

In the Andes the native peasant predominates. He is subject to the process of migration from rural areas into the towns and is consequently becoming more "mixed" in race.

Technological progress is threatening the survival of ethno-cultural minorities, such as the Cayapas, the Colorados (a tribe in an advanced state of acculturation), and other forest-dwelling tribes of Oriente, and thus their specific cultural features.

The population of Ecuador is not very evenly distributed throughout the territory; there is a concentration in some areas, while others are very sparsely populated.

A GLIMPSE OF THE PAST

As a result of systematical anthropological research it can be asserted that Ecuador has behind it at least 12,000 years of civilization. This does not means that there are no older remains, but that there is coherent archaeological evidence covering the PRE-CERAMIC period, from the tenth to the fourth millenium B.C.. The chief characteristics of the epoch were semi-nomadic tribes of predatory human beings who lived mainly by hunting and gathering fruit. The El Inga site near Quito is the most representative of this period, which is also known as the Paleo-Indian.

The PRIMARY Period began in 3200 B.C., when men began to cultivate the soil, which tended to make them more sedentary. Within this period there was the Valdivia stage, which produced the first ceramic culture in the New World. Mention should here be made of the anthropomorphous statuettes known as the Valdivia "Venuses".

The Machalilla and Chorrera phases also form part of the PRIMARY period. In the Chorrera culture there appear the "whistle-bottles" - a sort of jug which makes musical sounds when the air inside it is displaced by the liquid contained in the receptacle.

In 500 B.C. there began a new period known as that of REGIONAL DEVELOPMENT, which was to last until the fifth century A.D.. During these thousand years we can distinguish the Changala, Bahia, Jama-Coaque, Tolita, Marrio II, Penzalec I and Tuncahan cultures.

This period produced articles of pottery and metalwork of great aesthetic value. To quote only one example, during the phase of Tolita culture, platinum was being worked two thousand five hundred years ago, whereas in Europe it was not being used until the eighteenth century.

Between the fifth and fifteenth centuries A.D. there occurred the INTEGRATION period, within which we can distinguish the Milagro-Quevedo, Manteño, Jama Coaque II, Tacalshapa, Cashaloma, Panzaleo II and III, Puruha, Negativo-del-Carchi and Cuasmal stages of culture.

This brings us to the period of resistance against DOMINATION BY THE INCAS, which was to last about sixty years and chiefly affected the Ecuadorian Sierra. A sun temple at Ingapirca in Cañar Province bears witness to this period; it is the most impressive architectural work of the Incas in our country. Quito became the second capital of the Tahuantinsuyo. It would be wrong to suppose that the whole of the past history of Ecuador is tied up with the Incas, since the actual period of Inca domination was very short, as we have seen. This misunderstanding was spread by the early Indian chroniclers, and unfortunately it still persists.

The main feature of the history of the sixteenth century was the discovery, conquest and colonization of America by Europe, in which Spain played a leading part. One result of the colonial period was the ethnic and cultural intermingling which is characteristic of Ecuador today. In spite of the profound social injustices of the period, the Colony produced sculptures and pictures which together make up the so-called "Colonial Art". In 1542 Francisco de Orellana, at the head of an expedition organized and financed by Quito, discovered the River Amazon.

On 10 August 1809, the first claims to American Independence rang out through Quito. On 24 May 1822, after the battle of Pichincha in which Antonio José de Sucre, lieutenant of Simon Bolivar the Liberator, took part, the country was annexed to Greater Colombia. In 1830 there began the republican epoch.

As from 1972 Ecuador, which had hitherto been an exporter of agricultural produce, became an exporter of minerals too. It was the presence of petroleum which was to modify labour relations in industry and thus the entire course of history. The New World was to become a changed world.

ECONOMIC ASPECTS

The basis of the Ecuador economy is what is known as the primary sector. Agriculture is the dominant activity; a distinction should be made between agriculture for export and that for domestic consumption.

The main agricultural products exported are bananas, coffee and cocoa.

The economy of the country largely depends on foreign trade. Cocoa exports were at their height during the years from 1880 to 1920. Bananas attained their zenith during the decade from 1950 to 1960.

Agriculture, forestry and fishing account for about 40% of the Gross National Product, with manufactured goods accounting for 16%. The Gross National Product in 1972 was $ US 1,776 million and rose to 4.204 million in 1975. The chief industries are food products and textiles, in addition to these there are chemical and pharmaceutical products, paper pulp and paper as such, iron and steel, precision engineering, electronics, metal working, cement, sugar, tobacco and so on. Annual per capita revenue in Ecuador is about $ US 600.

The entire petroleum industry, including the State refinery at Esmeraldas, constitutes a new factor in the national economy, for every day 210,000 barrels are transported by the trans-Ecuador pipeline running from Lake Agrio in Oriente province to the tanker harbour of Balao in the Province of Esmeraldas. The "Corporación Estatal Petrolera Ecuadoriana" (CEPE) holds 62.5 % of the Organization of Petroleum-Exporting Countries (OPEC). The country receives nearly 12 Dollars per barrel of oil exported.

Firms operating in Ecuador find that it is extremely profitable. With a view to economic integration and expansion of its markets, our country forms part of the Andean Pact, together with Venezuela, Colombia, Peru and Bolivia.

Resources in fish, timber reserves and mineral wealth constitute an advantageous potential for the intensive, harmonious development of the national economy.

The extraordinary tourist attractions of Ecuador, revealed in the illustrations to this book, speak for themselves.

To conclude this rapid sketch of the Ecuadorian economy, the currency is stable.

CULTURAL ASPECTS

The cultural heritage of Ecuador is distinguished by its originality and wealth. The symbiosis of European Graeco-Roman culture with the roots of the native culture produced an Andean barock which takes concrete shape in the churches and monasteries which are rightly considered as the best of the Continent. San Francisco (sixteenth century) and La Compañia (seventeenth century) are eloquent examples of this. The renowned "Escuela Quitaña" produced artists such as Pampite, Legarda, Caspicara, Miguel de Santiago, Goribar and Sangurima, to name only the most outstanding.

The plastic tradition is still strong. In painting, for example, we have such remarkable artists as Oswaldo Guayasamin, Manuel Rendon Semanario, Eduardo Kingman, Enrique Tabara, Oswaldo Viteri, Muis Molinari, Estuardo Maldonado and Anibal Villacia, all of whom produce work which is as fecund as it is varied and occupies pride of place among contemporary Latin-American plastic art products.

So far as literature is concerned, the famous "Guayaquil Group", with Callegos Lara, De La Cuadra, Parejo Dieszcanseco, Aguilera Malta and Gil Gilbert holds its place among Latin-American writers.

I shall merely mention Angel Felicisimo Rojas and Jorge Icaza as novelists and Jorge Enrique Adoum as poets.

Benjamin Carrion is the major force behind contemporary literary production.

Activities such as the theatre, ballet, music and a national cinema still have a long way to go.

Juan CUEVA Jaramillo

GEOGRAPHISCHE GEGEBENHEITEN

Im Nordwesten von Südamerika gelegen, wird Ecuador im Norden von Kolumbien, im Osten und Süden von Peru und im Westen vom Pazifischen Ozean begrenzt.

Es besitzt drei näturliche- ekologisch verschiedene- Regionen: die "Costa", die Sierra und den "Oriente". Tausend Kilometer von der Küste entfernt liegen die Galapagos-Inseln, die eine Provinz Ecuadors bilden.

Die ecuadorianischen Anden teilen sich in zwei Ketten: die östliche und die westliche, die dem Land ein doppeltes Rückgrat aus Eis, Lava und Granit verleiht.

Costa. Fruchtbare Ebenen erstrecken sich zwischen der westlichen Kordillere und dem Pazifischen Ozean. Siebzigtausend Quadratkilometer, die sich auf fünf Provinzen verteilen: Esmeraldas, Manabi, Guayas, Los Rios und El Oro.

Das Klima ist warm und feucht; sein Boden erzeugt Bananen, Kaffee, Kakao, Zuckerrohr, Reis, die verschiedenartigsten Früchte und zahlreiche Hölzer, die zum grössten Teil dem Aussenhandel zugutekommen.

Das tropische Klima der Costa und die senkrechten Sonnenstrahlen werden von der kalten und wohltuenden Humboldtstromüng gemildert. Es existieren zwei Jahreszeiten: eine warme und regenreiche, die man paradoxerweise Winter nennt (von Dezember bis Mai) und eine trockene und weniger warme, die Sommer genannt wird (von Juni bis November). Die Durchschnittstemperatur schwankt zwischen 26 und 29° C.

Die wasserreichen Flussysteme des Guayas, des Esmeraldas und des Santiagos bewässern die Böden und dienen als Transportstrassen.

Guayaquil, grösster Hafen und industrielles Entwicklungszentrum, ist die bevölkertste Stadt des Landes (ungefähr 850 000 Einwohner).

Die Sierra. Die Hochebenen bedecken eine Oberfläche von 72 000 Quadratkilometern. Der interandische Übergang wird von Querschranken unterbrochen, die hohe Becken bilden; er ist ebenfalls mit der panamerikanischen Landstrasse verbunden, die einen Triumph des Menschen über die Natur darstellt. Die Sierra setzt sich aus folgenden Provinzen zusammen: Carchi, Imbabura, Pichincha, Cotopaxi, Tungurahua, Bolivar, Chimborasso, Canar, Azuay und Loja.

Vulkane und Gebirge sind richtiggehende tellurische Symphonien von Felsen und Schnee in der ecuadorianischen Sierra. Der Chimborasso liegt 6.310 Meter über dem Meeresspiegel, der Cotopaxi ist über 6.000 Meter hoch und der Sangay (5.323 Meter) ist einer der aktivsten Vulkane der Erde.

Die Bodenbearbeitung wird fast ausschliesslich von der Eingeborenenbevölkerung ausgeübt; sie benutzt noch die althergebrachten Techniken. Die Erzeugnisse sind: Mais, Kartoffeln, Getreide und sonstige für den eigenen Verbrauch bestimmte Produkte. Die ländliche Modernisierung schreitet ständig fort. Die Durchschnittstemperatur beträgt 15° C.

Quito, die Hauptstadt der Republik, liegt 2.800 Meter über dem Meeresspiegel; der Stadtplan verläuft zwischen den Falten des Pichincha und stellt so eine einladende und ungewöhnliche Topographie dar. Politisches und Verwaltungszentrum des Landes, hat sie seit fünf Jahren ein erhebliches, wirtschaftliches Schwergewicht erhalten, und zwar dank der Entwicklung der Erdölindustrie und der Erweiterung des öffentlichen wirtschaftlichen Sektors.

Die anderen Städte der interandischen Zone sind: Cuenca, Universitätsstadt und kulturelles Zentrum, die, bevölkerungsmässig, die dritte des Landes ist. Ambato, Riobamba, Loja, Ibarra und viele andere, weniger wichtige, sind ein typisches Beispiel für den städtischen Wachstumsprozess auf Kosten des ländlichen Sektors.

Der Oriente. Ein vielversprechendes Gebiet für die Zukunft; mit üppiger Vegetation, einem tropischen, amazonischen Klima, verschiedenartigster Fauna: Der nur schwach bevölkerten Zone fehlt es noch an einer genügenden Infrastruktur, die eine fortdauernde Entwicklung seines Wirtschaftspotentiels möglich machen würde. Die Bevölkerung des Oriente besteht aus Fortswirtschaft treibenden Gruppen wie die Cofanes, die Sionas, die Secoyas, die Zaparos, die Canelos, die Yumbos, die Aucas, die Shuaras, die Jivaros und andere menschliche Gruppen mit primitiver sozialer Struktur.

Das nordöstliche Gebiet erzeugt augenblicklich über 200.000 Tonnen Erdöl, was Ecuador zum zweitgrössten südamerikanischen Ausfuhrland von Kohlenwasserstoffverbindungen macht.

Die Provinzen Napo, Pastaza, Morona-Santiago und Zamora-Chinchipe sind noch ein Magma, aus dem sich Wirklichkeit und Versprechungen, Möglichkeiten und Herausforderungen herauskristallisieren.

Galapagos. Tausend Kilometer von der ecuadorianischen Küste entfernt, befindet sich der Colon Archipel oder Galapagos-Inseln; sie verdanken ihren Namen den Riesenschildkröten oder "Galapagos" (geochelone elephantopus).

Die Galapagos-Inseln, mit ihrem Granit- und Lavaunterbau, sind ein wundervolles natürliches Laboratorium. Ihre Fauna steht einzigartig in der Welt dar. Im XVII. Jahrhundert dienten diese Inseln Piraten und Freibeutern als Unterschlupf. 1853 studiert Charles Darwin die Tiergattungen der Inseln und stellt seine Entwicklungstheorie auf, die sämtliche wissenschaftlichen Gegebenheiten seiner Zeit umstürzt. Die Angleichung an die Umgebung und die natürliche Auswahl sind Hypothesen, die zu jener Zeit leidenschaftliche Entgegnungen herausforderten.

Jetzt hat die ecuadorianische Regierung diese Inseln zum Nationalpark erklärt, was ihnen Schutz verleiht. Auf der Insel Santa Cruz beschützt die Station "Charles Darwin" diesen Schatz der ganzen Wissenschaft.

Die Galapagos-Inseln, diese seltsame Welt, die aus der Vergangenheit emporragt, ist ein Mahnzeichen für den Menschen, dieses schädliche Säugetier, damit er ein gerechtes ekologisches Gleichgewicht bewahre.

Die Bevölkerung. Nach der Volkszählung von 1974 - und eine jährliche Wachstumsrate von 3,4 % miteinbegriffen - zählt Ecuador ungefähr siebeneinhalb Millionen Einwohner, mit 22 Einwohnern pro Quadratkilometer.

Der historische Prozess hat eine allgemeine Rassenvermischung hervorgebracht, und man muss sich auf sozial-kulturelle Unterscheidungsmerkmale beziehen, wenn man die ethnischen Gruppen studieren will. Im Küstengebiet ist der Einfluss der Bauern "montuvio" vorwiegend, mit Ausnahme der Provinz Esmeraldas, die eine überwiegend schwarze Bevölkerung hat.

In den Anden ist der eingeborene Bauer vorherrschend; aber die ständige Abwanderung in die Städte bringt auch hier eine dauernd fortschreitende Rassenvermischung hervor.

Die ethnisch-kulturellen Minderheiten wie die Cayapas, die Colorados (in schon weit fortgeschrittener Akulturation begriffen), die Gruppen im östlichen Urwald, usw. sehen sich in ihrem Überleben und in ihrem spezifischen Kulturwesen durch den Fortschritt der technischen Gesellschaft bedroht.

Eine nur wenig harmonische demographische Verteilung, eine übermässige Konzentration in gewissen Zonen und eine nur schwache Bevölkerungsdichte in anderen Zonen, sind charakteristisch für den nationalen ecuadorianischen Raum.

BLICK AUF DIE VERGANGENHEIT

Dank schematisch unternommenen anthropologischen Studien können wir feststellen, dass Ecuador eine 12.000 Jahre alte Kultur besitzt. Was nicht etwa heissen soll, dass es nicht auch sogar ältere Überbleibsel gäbe. Aber zusammenhängende archäologische Dokumente führen uns 12.000 Jahre zurück, und zwar in die präkeramische Epoche. Diese erstreckt sich vom 10. bis ins 4. Jahrtausend vor unserer Zeitrechnung. Charakteristisch für diese Epoche sind Menschen, die in halbnomadischen Gruppen lebten; sie betrieben hauptsächlich Jagd und sammelten Früchte ein. Die Stätte El Inga, in der Nähe von Quito, ist besonders typisch für diese Periode, die auch unter dem Namen paleo-indische Periode bekannt ist.

3.200 Jahre vor unserer Zeitrechnung beginnt die Primär-Periode, in der der Mensch anfängt, den Boden zu bestellen, was zu einem höheren Grad von Sesshaftigkeit führt. Von dieser Periode sticht die Valdivia-Phase ab, die die erste keramische Kultur der Neuen Welt war. Hier seien besonders die anthropomorphen Figuren erwähnt, die als Venusfiguren von Valdivia bekannt sind.

Die Phasen Machalilla und Chorrera gehören ebenfalls der Primärepoche an. In der Chorrera-Kultur erscheinen die Flaschenpfeifen; das sind Keramikgefässe, die musikalische Laute von sich geben, wenn die in ihnen enthaltene Flüssigkeit die Luft verdrängt:

500 Jahre vor unserer Zeitrechnung beginnt eine neue REGIONALE ENTWICKLUNG genannte Epoche; diese erstreckt sich bis ins 5. Jahrhundert unserer Zeitrechnung. In diesen 1000 Jahren unterscheidet man folgende Phasen: Guangala, Bahia, Jama-Coaque, la Tolita, Narrio II, Panzaleo I und Tuncahuan.

Der fortgeschrittene esthetische Sinn der Menschen offenbart sich in ihren Keramik- und Metallarbeiten. Um nur ein Beispiel zu erwähnen, während der La Tolita - Phase arbeitete man schon seit 2.500 Jahren mit Platin, was in Europa erst im 18. Jahrhundert der Fall ist.

In die Zeitspanne zwischen dem 5. und dem 15. Jahrhundert unserer Zeitrechnung fällt die INTEGRATIONS-Periode, bei der man folgende kulturelle Phasen unterscheiden kann: Milagro-Quevedo, Manteno, Jama-Coaque II, Tacalshapa, Cashaloma, Panzaleo II und III, Puruha, Negativo-del-Carchi und Cuasmal.

Das ist die Periode der INKAHERRSCHAFT, die 60 Jahre andauert und besonders in der ecuadorianischen Sierra ausgeübt wird. In der Provinz Canar legt Ingapirca davon Zeugnis ab; das ist ein Sonnentempel, der das bedeutendste Inkabauwerk in unserem Lande ist. Quito wird die zweite Hauptstadt des Tahuantinsuyo. Es wäre ein Irrtum, unsere ganze Vergangenheit als inkagebunden anzusehen, da es sich da ja -wie wir gesehen haben- nur um einen kurzen Zeitabschnitt handelt. Verschiedene Historiker halten leider auch heute noch an diesem Irrtum fest.

Das 16. Jahrhundert ist gekennzeichnet durch die Entdeckung, die Eroberung und die Kolonisation Amerikas von Seiten Europas (Spanien spielt dabei eine wesentliche Rolle). Die Kolonialperiode erzeugte die ethnische und kulturelle Rassenmischung, die heute für Ecuador kennzeichnend ist. Die Kolonie - trotz der einschneidenden sozialen Ungerechtigkeiten dieser Epoche - bringt eine Bildhauer- und Malkunst hervor, die gerade unter dem Namen Kolonialkunst bekanntgeworden ist. Im Jahre 1542 entdeckt Francisco de Orellana den Amazonasstrom an der Spitze einer von Quito aus organisierten und finanzierten Expedition.

Am 10. August 1809 hallt in Quito der erste amerikanische Unabhängigkeitsruf wieder. Am 24. Mai 1822 -nach der Schlacht von Pichincha, an welcher Antonio José de Sucre, ein Kamerad des Befreiers Simon Bolivar, teilnimmt - schliesst sich das Land Gran Colombia an. 1830 beginnt die republikanische Epoche.

Ab 1972 wird Ecuador zu einem Ausfuhrland, das neben landwirtschaftlichen Erzeugnissen auch Metalle und Erze ausführt.

Erdölvorkommen verändern die sozialen Produktionsverhältnisse des Landes und dadurch den Verlauf seiner Geschichte. So wird die neu entdeckte Welt wirklich zu einer neuen Welt.

WIRTSCHAFTLICHE ASPEKTE

Die Basis der ecuadorianischen Wirtschaft ist der primäre Sektor. Die Landwirtschaft ist die hervorragendste Tätigkeit; einerseits werden die landwirtschaftlichen Produkte zur Ausfuhr benutzt und andererseits dienen sie für den eigenen Verbrauch.

Die wichtigsten Ausfuhrprodukte sind: Bananen, Kaffee und Kakao.

Die Wirtschaft des Landes hängt zum grössten Teil vom Aussenhandel ab. Der Höhepunkt der sogenannten Kakaoepoche wurde zwischen den Jahren 1880 und 1920 erreicht. Der Bananenhandel blühte besonders in den Jahren 1950 bis 1960.

Landwirtschaft, Fortstwirtschaft und Fischfang stellen ungefähr 40 % des Nationalprodukts, der Anteil der Manufakturerzeugnisse beträgt 16%. 1972 belief sich das Bruttonationalprodukt auf 1776 Millionen U.S. Dollar und wird 1975 auf 4204 Millionen Dollar ansteigen. Die vorwiegenden Industrien sind die Nahrungsmittel- und die Textilindustrie; ausserdem gibt es noch Industrien für chemische und Arzneiprodukte, die Industrie für Papierbrei- und Papierherstellung; die Eisen-und Stahlindustrie, Industrie für die Herstellung von Präzisionsapparaten, die elektronische Industrie, die Metall- und Zementindustrie, Zucker- und Tabakindustrie, usw. Das jährliche Einkommen pro Einwohner beträgt 600 U.S. Dollar.

Die ganze Erdölindustrie, die staatliche Raffinerie der Provinz Esmeraldas miteinbegriffen, stellt in der nationalen Wirtschaft eine neue Tatsache dar; tagtäglich wird eine Produktion von 210.000 Tonnen Erdöl von der transecuadorianischen Erdölleitung transportiert; Ausgangspunkt ist Lago Agrio in der Provinz Oriente, Endpunkt ist der Erdölhafen von Balao in der Provinz Esmeraldas. Die "Corporación Estatal Petrolera Ecuatoriana" -CEPE- besitzt 62,5% der Aktien des Erdölkonsortiums Texaco-Cepe. In seiner Eigenschaft als Erdölausfuhrland gehört Ecuador der Organisation der Erdöl ausführenden Länder an. Für jede ausgeführte Tonne Erdöl erhält das Land 12 Dollar.

Das Rentabilitätsniveau der in Ecuador arbeitenden Unternehmen ist durchaus positiv. Auf der Suche nach wirtschaftlicher Integration und nach neuen Märkten ist Ecuador dem berühmten Andenpakt beigetreten, dem auch Venezuela, Kolumbien, Peru und Bolivien angehören.

Der ichtyologische Reichtum, die Holzreserven und die Bodenschätze stellen ein interessantes Potential dar, das auf eine intensive und harmonische Entwicklung der nationalen Wirtschaft schliessen lässt.

Die aussergewöhnliche touristische Anziehungskraft Ecuadors spricht für sich selbst: die Photos in diesem Album legen dafür ein beredtes Zeugnis ab.

Zur Ergänzung dieses kurzen Überblicks über die ecuadorianische Wirtschaft sei noch auf die Währungsstabilität des Landes hingewiesen.

KULTURELLE ASPEKTE

Der ecuadorianische Kulturschatz zeichnet sich durch seine Originalität und seinen Reichtum aus. Die Symbiose der europäischen griechisch-lateinischen Kultur mit den kulturellen Wurzeln des Eingeborenentums hat den andischen Barock hervorgebracht, der in den Kirchen und Klöstern seinen Niederschlag findet. Diese werden mit Recht als die schönsten des Kontinents betrachtet. San Francisco -XVI. Jahrhundert- und die Compania -XVIII. Jahrhundert- sind dafür beredte Beispiele. Die berühmte "Escuela Quitena" brachte Künstler wie Pampite, Legarda, Caspicara, Miguel de Santiago, Goribar, Sangurima hervor, um nur die berühmtesten zu erwähnen.

Die plastischen Künste zeugen immer noch von der Tradition. In der Malerei, zum Beispiel, verfügt das Land über so bemerkenswerte Schöpfer wie Oswaldo Guayasamin, Manuel Rendon Semanario, Eduardo Kingman, Enrique Tabara, Oswaldo Viteri, Luis Molinari, Estuardo Maldonado, Anibal Villacis, die eine mannigfache und fruchtbare Kunst hervorgebracht haben; diese nimmt im Rahmen der zeitgenössischen südamerikanischen plastischen Künste eine hervorragende Stellung ein.

Was die Schriftsteller anbetrifft, deren Tradition auf den Indianer Espejo, in der Kolonialzeit, Zurückgeht, so sei hier besonders auf die "Grupo de Guayaquil" hingewiesen, der Gallegos Lara, De La Cuadra, Pareja Diezcanseco, Aguilera Malta und Gil Gilbert angehören; diese Schriftsteller können mit den besten des Kontinents wetteifern.

Hier seien noch die Romanschriftsteller Angel Felicisimo Rojas und Jorge Icaza angeführt, sowie die Dichter Cesar Davila Andrade, Gonzalo Escudero, Jorge Carrera Andrade und Jorge Enrique Adoum.

Benjamin Carrion gibt der zeitgenössischen Literatur ihren besonderen Auftrieb.

Die soziale Forschung ist in einer vollständigen Umwälzung begriffen. Theater, Tanz, Musik und das nationale Filmwesen stehen erst am Anfang eines langen, aber Erfolg versprechenden Wegs.

Juan CUEVA Jaramillo

Pagina 25 26

Vasija Zoomorfa. Transición entre las fases culturales Tacalshapa y Cashaloma. Período de Integración. Siglo V al XV d.C.

Figura antropomorfa de la fase cultural Negativo-Del-Carchi. Período de Integración. Siglo V al XV d.C.

Figura antropomorfa de la fase cultural Jama-Coaque. Período de Desarrollo Regional. 500 a.C. 500 d.C.

Page 24 25 26

Poterie zoomorphe - Transition entre les phases culturelles Tacalshapa et Cashaloma - Période d'Intégration - Vème au XVème siècle après J.C.

Figure anthropomorphe de la phase culturelle Negativo-Del-Carchi - Période d'Intégration - Vème au XVème siècle après J.C.

Figure anthropomorphe de la phase culturelle Jama-Coaque - Période de Développement Régional - 500 avant J.C. à 500 après J.C.

Page 24 25 26

Zoomorphous pottery - transition between Tacalshapa and Cashaloma stages of culture - integration period - fifth and sixth centuries A.D..

Anthropomorphous figure of the Negativo-Del-Carchi stage of culture - Integration period - fifth and sixth centuries A.D..

Anthropomorphous figure of the Jama-Coaque stage of culture - regional development period - 500 B.C. to 500 A. D...

Seite 24 25 26

Zoomorphes Geschirr - Übergang zwischen den kulturellen Phasen Tacalshapa und Cashaloma. 5. oder 6. Jahrhundert nach J. Chr.

Anthropomorphe Figur der kulturellen Phase Negativo-Del-Carchi - Integrationsperiode - 5. oder 6. Jahrhundert nach J. Chr.

Anthropomorphe Figur der kulturellen Phase Jama-Coaque - Regionale Entwicklungsperiode - 500 vor J. Chr. bis 500 nach J. Chr.

Figuras utilizadas para arreglar los Nacimientos. Arte quiteño del Siglo XVIII. Anónimos.

Statuettes utilisées dans les crèches. Art quiténien du XVIIIème siècle. Anonyme.

Statuettes used for nativity scenes. Eighteenth century Quito art. Anonymous.

Für Krippen benutzte Figürchen. Quito-Kunst, aus dem 18. Jahrhundert. Anonym.

La Dormición de la Virgen. Siglo XVIII. Monasterio del Carmen Alto - Quito.

La dormition de la Vierge. XVIIIème siècle. Monastère du Haut Carmel. Quito.

The sleeping Virgin. Upper Carmelite Monastery in old Quito.

Schlafende Jungfrau. 18. Jahrhundert. Kloster im Oberen Carmel.

Angel de Legarda - Quito.

Ange de Legarda. Quito.

Legarda angel - Quito.

Ein Engel Legardas - Quito.

La imaginería colonial nos presenta una talla policromada obra del indio Manuel Chili, conocido como Caspicara - Siglo XVIII.

L'imagerie coloniale nous présente une sculpture polychrome de l'indien Manuel Chili connu sous le nom de Caspicara. XVIIIème siècle.

Colonial plastic arts. Polychrome sculpture by the Indian, Manuel Chili, known as Caspicara eighteenth century.

Kolonialbildkunst, polychrome Skulptur des Indianers Manuel Chili, bekannt unter dem Namen Caspicara - 18. Jahrhundert.

La expresión serena de un rostro se descascara en esta muestra de la imaginería popular.

La sérénité d'un visage surgit de cet échantillon de l'imagerie populaire.

The calm expression of a face in this example of popular imagery.

Volksbildkunst... ein Ruhe ausdrückendes Antlitz.

← *Trabajo humano y pan de oro a raudales en la capilla de Cantuña. Bernardo de Legarda - Siglo XVIII.*

← *Travail humain et feuille d'or à profusion dans la chapelle de Cantuña - Bernardo de Legarda. XVIIIème siècle.*

← *Human labour and a profusion of gold leaf in the Cantuna Chapel - Bernardo de Legarda - eighteenth century.*

← *In der Kapelle von Cantuna - ein Werk Bernardo de Legardas, das mit Goldblättchen bedeckt ist - 18. Jahrhundert.*

← *La Dolorosa de Caspicara. Museo de Arte Colonial - Quito.*

← *Vierge aux Douleurs de Capiscara, Musée d'Art Colonial. Quito.*

← *Caspicara's Mater Dolorosa. Museum of Colonial Art - Quito.*

← *Die Dolorosa Caspicaras. Museum für Kolonialkunst - Quito.*

Ingapirca, provincia de Cañar. Templo al Sol (antes de su restauración). Período de Dominación Incaica.

Ingapirca, Province de Cañar, temple du Soleil (avant sa restauration). Epoque de la domination Inca.

Ingapirca in Canar province. Sun Temple (before restoration). Period of the Inca domination.

Ingapirca, Provinz Canar. Ein Sonnentempel (vor seiner Restauration). Periode der Inkaherrschft.

Monumento a la línea equinoccial, cerca de Cayambe, provincia de Pichincha.

Monument, rappelant le passage de la ligne de l'Equateur, province de Pichincha, près de Cayambe.

Monument at the equator, near Cayambe in Pichincha Province.

Ein Denkmal zur Erinnerung an die Überschreitung der Äquatorlinie, Provinz Pichincha, der Nähe von Cayambe.

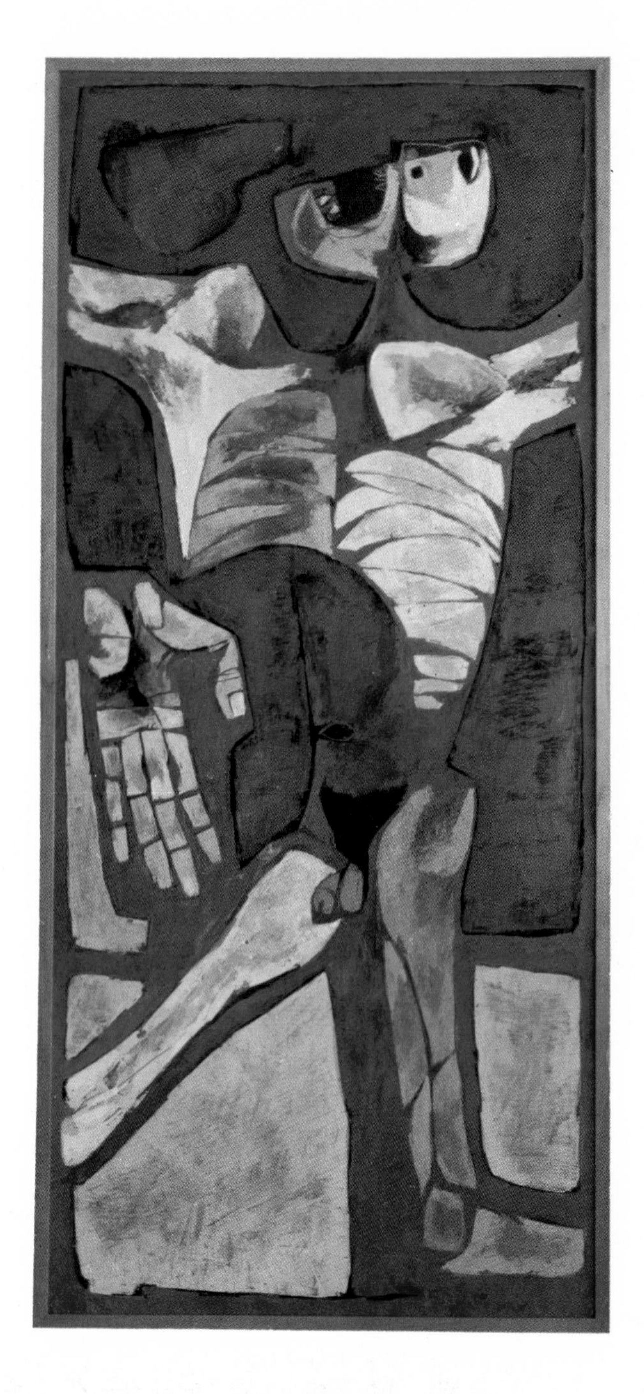

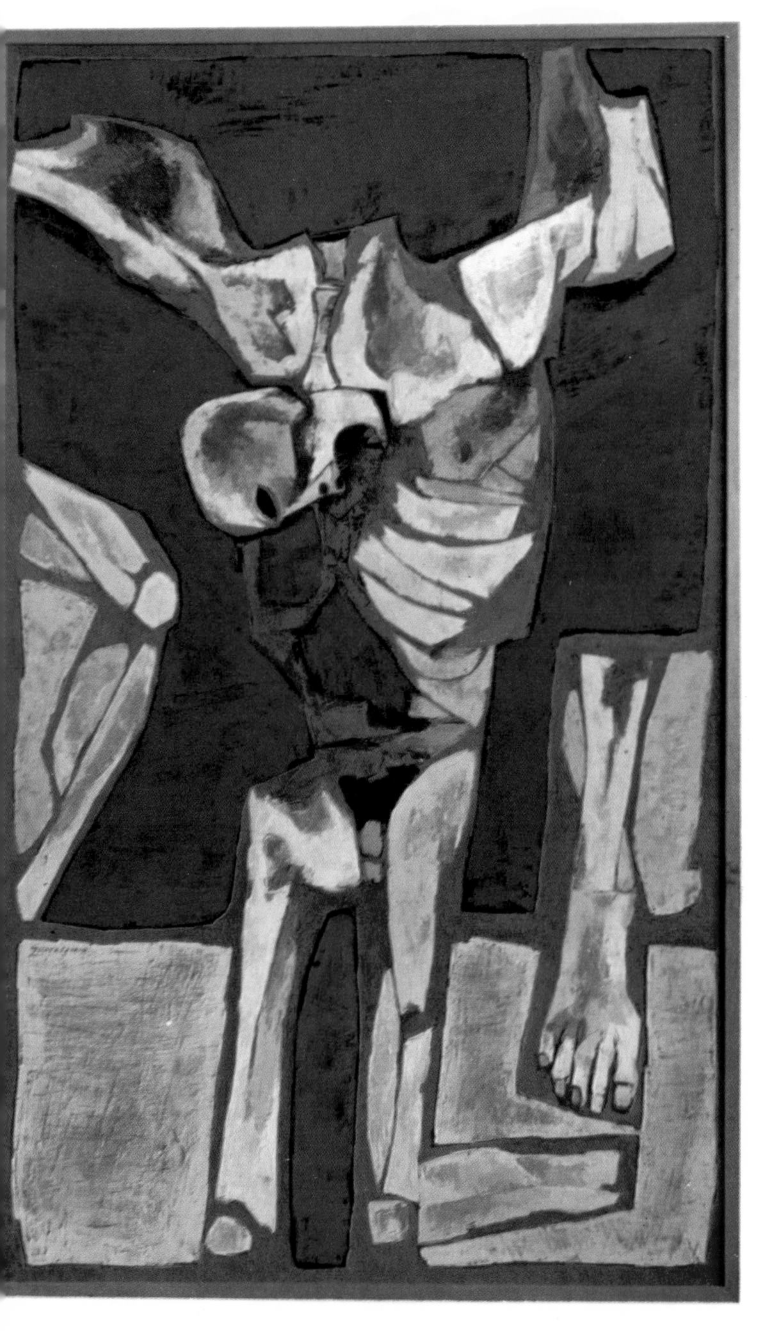

Los raíces aborígenes pesan en la pintura de Oswaldo Guayasamín, una figura de la plástica latinoamericana actual. Los Andes se universalizan a través de creadores como este notable pintor ecuatoriano.

Les racines aborigènes prédominent dans la peinture d'Oswaldo Guayasamin, un maître des arts plastiques latino-américains contemporains. Les Andes acquièrent un rayonnement universel grâce à des artistes comme ce remarquable peintre équatorien.

Aboriginal roots dominate the painting of Oswaldo Guayasamin, one of the masters of contemporary Latin-American plastic art. The atmosphere imparted by the creations of this remarkable Ecuadorian painter renders the Andes universal.

Die Eingeborenenkunst beeinflusst die Malerei von Oswaldo Guayasamin, einer der Meister der bildenden, lateinamerikanischen Künste. Die Anden üben so einen universellen Einfluss aus, dank Künstlern wie dieser ausgezeichnete ecuadorianische Maler.

Quito, la capital, incursiona en terrenos del Pichincha, volcán adormecido e impresionante.

Quito, la capitale, s'insinue dans les replis du Pichincha, impressionnant volcan endormi.

Quito, the capital, stretches out into the foothills of the Pichincha, an impressive volcano which is now extinct.

Die Hauptstadt Quito stösst bis zum Pichincha, dem eindrucksvollen, jetzt erloschenen Vulkan, vor.

Quito, a 2.800 m. sobre el nivel del mar, no le teme a la modernización.

Quito à 2.800 m au-dessus du niveau de la mer, ne craint pas le modernisme.

Quito, at 9,500 feet above sea level, is not afraid of the twentieth century.

Quito, 2.800 m über dem Meeresspiegel gelegen, fürchtet den Modernismus nicht.

SACRUM

← *Iglesia de La Compañía, siglo XVIII, Quito. Un encaje en piedra bordado con las normas del barroco tardío.*

← *Calle La Ronda en Quito. El tiempo se ha detenido en una arquitectura de proporciones humanas. Balcones, aleros y faroles nos hablan del viejo mundo.*

Plaza Grande, monumento a la Independencia y palacio de Gobierno bajo un cielo luminoso.

← *Eglise de la Compagnie, XVIIIème siècle, Quito. Dentelle de pierre travaillée selon les canons d'un baroque tardif.*

← *Rue La Ronda, à Quito. Le temps s'est arrêté dans une architecture aux proportions humaines. Balcons, auvents et lanternes nous parlent de l'ancien monde.*

La Grande Place, Monument de l'Indépendance et Palais du Gouvernement sous un ciel lumineux.

← *The eighteenth-century Church of La Compania at Quito. Lacework of stone carved in accordance with the late Barock style.*

← *Quito - the Calle La Ronda. Time stands still in this architecture with its human proportions. Balconies, terraces and lantern tell us of a forgotten world.*

The main square: the independence monument and the seat of Government under a luminous sky.

← *Die Kirche "de La Compañia", 18. Jahrhundert - Quito. Ein mit Borten versehenes steinernes Spitzenwerk gemäss den Regeln des Spätbarocks.*

← *Die Strasse "La Ronda" in Quito. Hier hielt die Zeit an. Eine Architektur mit menschlichen Proportionen. Balkone und Laternen erzählen uns von einer vergangenen Welt.*

Der "Plaza Grande", das Unabhängigkeitsdenkmal und der Regierungspalast unter strahlendem Himmel.

El paisaje humaniza a este conjunto multifamiliar. Quito.

Le paysage humanise ce complexe d'habitation. Quito.

This group of dwellings in Quito is humanized by the surrounding landscape.

Die Landschaft vermenschlicht diesen Wohnkomplex in Quito.

El paso del tiempo al pulso de la arquitectura quiteña.

La marche du temps au rythme de l'architecture de Quito.

Time marching at the pace of Quito architecture.

Der Lauf der Zeit im Rythmus der Architektur von Quito.

Se escucha el silencio en el patio y los corredores del claustro de San Agustín. Quito.

On écoute le silence dans le jardin et dans les galeries du cloître de San Agustin, Quito.

You learn to listen to silence again in this patio and in the corridors of the San Agustin cloister.

Im Klostergarten und in den Gängen des Klosters von San Agüstin hört man dem Schweigen zu. Quito.

Banco Central. Quito. El edificio alberga el mejor museo arqueológico del país.

Banque Centrale. Quito. L'édifice abrite le plus important musée archéologique du pays, et, un des plus beaux d'Amérique du Sud.

Quito, the Central Bank. The building contains the most extensive archaeological museum in the country.

Die Zentralbank - Quito. In diesem Gebäude befindet sich das bedeutendste archäologische Museum des Landes, das zugleich eines der schönsten ganz Südamerikas ist.

Monasterio de Guápulo, reliquia arquitectónica inmersa en un paisaje fascinante.

Monastère de Guapulo, joyau architectural au coeur d'un paysage fascinant.

Guapulo Monastery, an architectural jewel set in a fascinating landscape.

Das Kloster von Guapulo, ein Kleinod der Architektur, das inmitten einer faszinierenden Landschaft versteckt liegt.

El hotel Quito, arquitectura moderna enmarcada entre altas y verdes montañas - muchas de ellas coronadas de nieve. Cada habitación cuenta con un balcón desde donde se aprecia una excitante vista en cualquier dirección.

L'hôtel Quito, architecture moderne au coeur de hautes et vertes montagnes. Plusieurs d'entre elles enneigées. Chaque chambre est dotée d'un balcon d'où l'on peut admirer les environs.

The Quito Hotel, modern architecture surrounded by lofty, verdant mountains, many of which are snow-covered. Each room has a balcony from which the surrounding countryside can be seen.

Das Hotel Quito, eine moderne Architektur im Herzen der hohen und grünen Berge, von denen mehrere mit Schnee bedeckt sind. Jedes Zimmer hat einen Balkon, von dem aus man die Umgebung bewundern kann.

Las naves multicolores de la empresa estatal Ecuatoriana de Aviación llevan un mensaje de amistad desde la mitad del mundo a los pueblos de América y a todos los países del orbe.

The multi-coloured aircraft of "Ecuatoriana de Aviación", the State Airline, bring a message of friendship from across the world to the peoples of America and to all countries of the world.

El aeropuerto internacional Mariscal Sucre, en Quito, recibe un tráfico aereo cada vez más intenso.

Compañias aereas como Branif, Air France, Aereo Peru, Avianca, conectan el Ecuador con el resto del mundo.

El servicio interno es atentido por companias nacionales tales como Saeta, Tame, San, etc...

El Hotel Colón, en el mismo centro, es de clase internacional. En Quito existe un problema de alojamiento y los hoteles siempre están llenos. De modo a resolver este problema, el hotel Colón acaba de construir un nuevo edificio, por lo cual su capacidad pasa a 450 habitaciones en lugar de 200, así como un centro internacional de convenciones. En la capital existen tres casinos, uno en el hotel Humbolt, otro en el hotel Quito, y otro, como lo pueden ver en esta foto, en el hotel Colón.

L'Hôtel Colon, en plein centre, est de classe internationale. Il existe à Quito un problème d'accueil et les hôtels sont toujours complets. Pour résoudre ce problème, l'hôtel Colon vient de construire un nouvel édifice qui porte sa capacité de 200 à 450 chambres, ainsi qu'un centre international de congrès. Il y a trois casinos dans la capitale; l'un à l'hôtel Humboldt, l'autre à l'hôtel Quito, le troisième, comme on peut le voir ci-dessous, à l'hôtel Colon.

The Colon Hotel in the centre of the city is in the international class. Quito has an accomodation problem, and hotels are always full. In an attempt to solve this problem, the Colon Hotel has just built an annex which will increase its capacity from 200 to 450 rooms, together with an international congress centre. There are three casinos in the capital - one at the Humboldt, one at the Quito and the third, shown below, at the Colon Hotel.

Das Hotel Colon, mitten im Zentrum gelegen, ist von internationaler Klasse. Es gibt in Quito ein Unterkunftsproblem, da die Hotels immer voll besetzt sind. Um dieses Problem zu lösen, hat das Hotel Colon ein neues Gebäude errichtet, wodurch die Zimmerkapazität von 200 auf 450 ansteigen wird. Das neue Hotel umfasst ebenfalls Konferenzsäle für internationale Veranstaltungen. Es gibt in der Hauptstadt drei Kasinos: eins im Hotel Humboldt, ein anderes im Hotel Quito und -untenstehend- das dritte, im Hotel Colon.

El "Flotel Orellana", un hotel flotante para descubrir una de las regiones más extraordinarias del planeta, la hoya amazonica. Con sus 180 toneladas ofrece comodidades de primera clase para 54 pasajeros.

El flotel Orellana, cuyo nombre deriva del descubridor del Amazonas, desciende el río Napo y permite vivir momentos inolvidables en la jungla amazónica.

Guías especializados sirven a los viajeros que observan maravillados la naturaleza exuberante poblada de pájaros multicolores, monos, extraños insectos y hormigas con su increible organización bajo el interminable concierto de la selva.

Durante el viaje, se organizan excursiones que llevan el pasajero a navegar en canoas aborígenes, descubrir lagos, despertar tortugas y caimanes, pescar pirañas. Es un retorno a la naturaleza. Al caer la tarde, el regreso al flotel es una vuelta al confort del siglo XX.

Cada día conferencias con proyecciones permiten al turista comprender mejor este viaje al corazón de la selva.

Le "Flotel Orellana", un hôtel flottant qui permet de découvrir l'une des régions la plus extraordinaire de la planète, le bassin Amazonien.

Avec ses 180 tonnes, il offre un confort de première classe pour 54 passagers.

Le Flotel Orellana, dont le nom provient de celui qui découvrit l'Amazone, descend le fleuve Napo et permet de vivre des moments inoubliables dans la forêt amazonienne.

Des guides spécialisés sont à la disposition des voyageurs qui observent, émerveillés, la nature exubérante peuplée d'oiseaux multicolores, de singes, d'étranges insectes et de fourmis, avec leur incroyable organisation, au sein de l'interminable concert de la Selva.

Pendant le voyage, des excursions en pirogue sont organisées, qui permettent au voyageur de découvrir des lacs, réveiller les tortues et les caïmans et pêcher des pirañas. C'est un retour à la nature. Au coucher du soleil, rentrer au Flotel Orellana est un retour au confort du 20ème siècle.

Tous les jours des conférences, avec des projections, permettent au touriste de mieux comprendre ce voyage au cœur de la forêt.

The "Flotel Orellana" - a floating hotel which enables the visitor to discover one of the most extraordinary regions in the world, the Amazonian basin.

This 180-tonner provides first-class comfort for 54 passengers.

The "Flotel Orellana", the name of which is derived from that of the discoverer of the Amazon, sails down the Napo River and provides unforgettable experiences of the Amazonian jungle.

Specialized guides are available for tourists, who are amazed to observe this wonderful, exuberant nature populated by multi-coloured birds, monkeys, strange insects and the ants which, with unbelievable organization, work away to the sound of the interminable concert of the woods.

Throughout the voyage, excursions in aboriginal canoes are organized; these will enable you to discover lakes, awake tortoises and caimans from their sleep and fish for piranas. At sunset, you return to the Flotel Orellana and to the comfort of the twentieth century.

Every day, there are talks accompanied by projections of slides and films, which enable the tourist to gain a fuller understanding of his journey into the heart of the forest.

Das schwimmende Hotel Orellana gibt den Besuchern die Möglichkeit, eine der ausserordentlichen Gebiete dieser Erde zu entdecken: das Amazonasbecken.

Mit seinen 180 Tonnen bietet es einen erstklassigen Komfort für 54 Passagiere.

Das schwimmende Hotel Orellana, dessen Namen an den Entdecker des Amazonas erinnert, fährt den Napostrom hinunter; man verbringt auf ihm unvergessliche Augenblicke im amazonischen Urwald.

Spezialisierte Führer stehen den Reisenden zur Verfügung. Man kann so, verzückt, die überschwengliche Natur betrachten, in der es von vielfarbigen Vögeln, Affen, seltsamen Insekten und Ameisen wimmelt, gewiegt von dem nie endenden Konzert der Selva.

Während der Reise kann man bei Ausflügen in Eingeborenenbarken die Seen entdecken, Schildkröten und Krokodile aufwecken und "Piranas" fischen. Das ist wirklich ein "Zurück zur Natur", Wenn man dann bei Sonnenuntergang in das schwimmende Hotel Orellana zurückkehrt, findet man den Komfort des 20. Jahrhunderts wieder.

Täglich finden Konferenzen mit Bildvorführungen statt, die dem Touristen noch besser diese Reise ins Innere des Urwalds erläutern.

Rostro y manos de los Andes.

Visage et mains des Andes.

The face and hands of the Andes.

Gesicht und Hände in den Anden.

Corridas de toros a nivel internacional en la feria de diciembre. Quito.

Courses de taureaux, de classe internationale, pendant les fêtes de Quito au mois de décembre.

Bull fight of international class during the December fiesta at Quito.

Stierkämpfe von internationalem Niveau finden während der Dezemberfeste in Quito statt.

Armonía de tejados. Cuenca, tercera ciudad del país e importante centro de artesanías.

Harmonie des toits. Cuenca, troisième ville et important centre artisanal.

A symphony of roofs. Cuenca, the third city of Ecuador and an important centre of handicrafts.

Harmonie der Dächer... Cuenca, die drittwichtigste Stadt und bedeutendes Handwerkszentrum.

Orillas del Tomebamba, uno de los cuatro ríos de Cuenca.

Rives du Tomebamba, l'une des quatre rivières de Cuenca.

Banks of the Tomebamba, one of the four rivers of Cuenca.

Ufer des Tomebamba, einer der vier Flüsse Cuencas.

La lana se convierte en hilo con la ancestral técnica del huso manual. Cuenca.

De la laine au fil, selon la technique ancestrale du fuseau.

Wool is turned into yarn by means of the ancient method using the spindle.

Die Wolle wird zum Faden dank der schon von den Vorfahren angewandten Technik.

Los mal llamados «panama hats» se secan bajo el sol de Cuenca.

Chapeaux improprement dits "de Panama", séchant au soleil de Cuenca.

The hats wrongly known as "Panamas", drying in the sun at Cuenca.

Zu Unrecht "Panama" genannte Hüte trocknen in der Sonne Cuencas.

Baños, antesala del Oriente, aguas termales y orquídeas cerca de la ciudad de Ambato.

Baños, antichambre de l'Oriente; eaux thermales et orchidées, près de la ville d'Ambato.

Baños, the anti-chamber of Oriente; reputed for its spa and its orchids, near the town of Ambato.

Baños, Vorzimmer zum östlichen Gebiet, Thermalquellen und Orchideen, in der Nähe der Stadt Ambato.

Mercado popular. Cuenca.

Marché populaire. Cuenca.

Street market at Cuenca.

Markt in Cuenca.

Cholas cuencanas venden cuyes a la brasa (conejillos de Indias).

"Cholas" de Cuenca vendant des cochons d'Indes rôtis.

The "Cholas" of Cuenca selling (roasted guinea pigs).

Die "Cholas" von Cuenca verkaufen geröstete Meerschweinchen.

Paisaje, trabajo, campo y color en la serranía andina.

Paysage, travail, champs et couleurs dans les montagnes andines.

Landscape, work, fields and colours in the Andes.

Landschaft, Arbeit, Felder und Farben im andischen Gebirge.

Niño indio al rondador. Música en la serranía. Compañía en la soledad.

Enfant indien à la flûte de Pan. Musique des montagnes, compagne de solitude.

Indian child with pipes of Pan. Music of the mountains, companion in loneliness.

Indianerkind mit Panflöte. Musik auf den Bergen, Begleiterin in der Einsamkeit.

Tejer no es un juego para estos niños indios.

Tisser n'est pas un jeu pour ces enfants indiens.

Weaving is not a sport for Indian children,

Weben ist kein Spiel für diese Indianerkinder.

Hilando y pensando junto al totoral.

Filant et pensant près des roseaux.

Spinning and thinking near the bullrushes.

Nachdenkliches Spinnen in der Nähe des Schilfrohrs.

Nevado El Altar. Poema telúrico y sueño de andinistas.

Massif du Chimborazo. Poème tellurique et rêve d'andiniste.

The snow-covered peaks of the Chimborazo..
Geological poem and dream of an Andes mountaineer.

Der verschneite Gipfel des Chimborasso.
Tellurisches Gedicht und Traum eines Andenbewohners.

Rostros, máscaras y música tristes para fiestas alegres, paréntesis del rudo vivir del campesino.

Visages, masques et musique tristes pour des fêtes joyeuses, une parenthèse dans la vie rude du paysan.

Sad faces, masks and music for a joyful occasion. A moment of relief from the hard toil of the peasant.

Traurige Gesichter, Masken und Musik für fröhliches Spiel; ein kurzes Aufatmen im rüden Leben des Bauern.

Nieves eternas en Chimborazo. Llamingos en el Pajonal.

Neiges éternelles sur le Chimborazo. Lamas sur la prairie d'altitude.

The eternal snows of Chimborazo. Lamas on the upland pasture.

Ewiger Schnee auf dem Chimborasso und Lamas auf der Alp.

Todo un año de trabajo para el vestuario de un día.

Toute une année de travail pour le costume d'un jour.

An entire year of work for the clothes worn on one day.

Ein ganzes Jahr Arbeit für das Kostüm eines einzigen Tages.

Ambato, tierra de Juan Montalvo, uno de los polemistas más lúcidos que ha tenido el Ecuador.

Ambato, terre natale de Juan Montalvo, l'un des polémistes les plus brillants que l'Equateur ait connus.

Ambato, the birthplace of Juan Montalvo, one of the most brilliant polemists Ecuador has ever had.

Ambato, Geburtsort Juan Montalvos, einer der berühmtesten Polemiker Ecuadors.

Estación ferroviaria en Ambato, ciudad de la Sierra asentada en una región frutícola de clima agradable.

Gare d'Ambato, ville de la Cordillère, sise dans une région fruitière au climat agréable.

The railway station at Ambato, town of the Cordillera, in a fruit-growing region with a pleasant climate.

Der Bahnhof von Ambato, eine Stadt der Kordilleren in einem an Früchten reichen Gebiet gelegen mit angenehmem Klima.

Esperando el mundo nuevo.

Dans l'espoir d'un monde nouveau.

The hope of a new world.

In der Hoffnung auf eine neue Welt.

Feria de animales en un villorrio de los interandes. Las técnicas del regateo estrechan las relaciones humanas.

Foire au bétail dans un petit village des Andes. L'art du marchandage resserre les relations humaines.

Cattle market in a small village of the Andes. Haggling makes for intimitate human relations.

Tierjahrmarkt in einem kleinen Dorf der Anden. Die Technik des Handelns unterhält die menschlichen Beziehungen.

Valle del Chota: la población negra piensa, trabaja y baila.

Vallée de Chota (province de Imbabura), la population pense, travaille et danse.

The Chota Valley (Imbabura Province). The population meditates, works and dances.

Das Tal von Chota, in der Provinz Imbabura, die Bevölkerung denkt nach, arbeitet und tanzt.

Guayaquil. Actividad productiva junto al caudaloso Guayas.

Guayaquil. La ville est baignée par le fleuve Guayas, c'est la métropole économique du pays.

Guayaquil, with the Guayas River, the economic capital of the country.

Guayaquil. Die Stadt wird von dem Strom Guayas umspült; sie ist die wirtschaftliche Hauptstadt des Landes.

El café se seca al sol en una calle de Guayaquil.

Le café sèche au soleil, dans une rue de Guayaquil.

Coffee drying in the sun in a Guayaquil street.

Auf einer Strasse in Guayaquil trocknet der Kaffee in der Sonne.

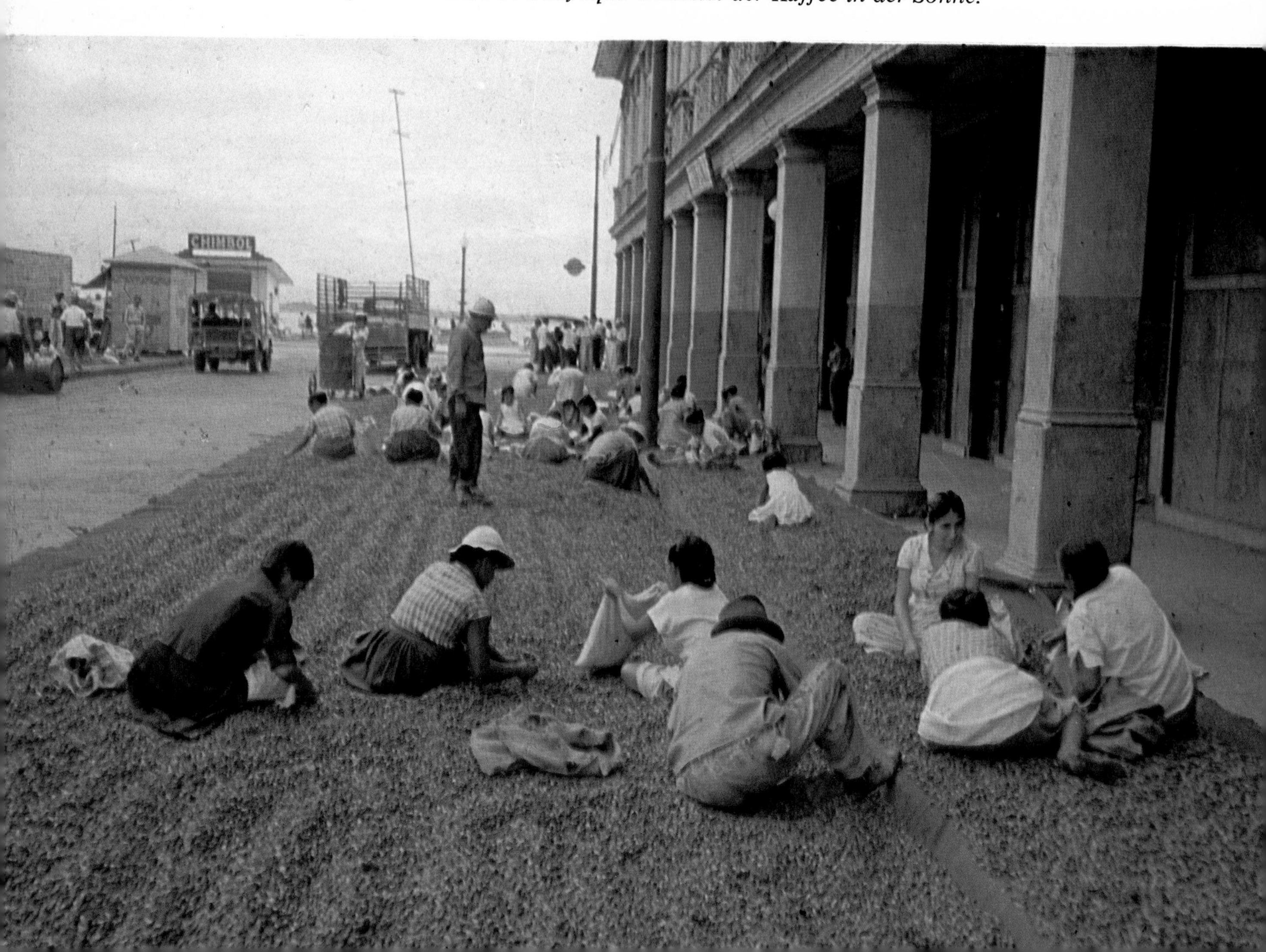

Cacao en Manta, un polo de desarrollo económico de la costa ecuatoriana.

Cacao à Manta, un des pôles du développement économique de la côte équatorienne.

Cocoa at Manta. One of the keys to the economic development of the Ecuador coast.

Kakao in Manta - einer der Stützpunkte der wirtschaftlichen Entwicklung der ecuadorianischen Küste.

Transporte de madera por un río de la costa.

Flottage du bois sur un fleuve de la côte.

Floating timber on a coastal river.

Holztransport auf einem Strom an der Küste.

Cortar madera es una faena solidaria con este tipo de sierra.

La nécessaire solidarité des scieurs de long.

The necessary solidarity of sawyers.

Holzsäger müssen aufeinander eingespielt sein.

Sinfonía en azul en un telar de Otavalo.

Symphonie en bleu sur un métier à tisser d'Otavalo.

Symphony in blue on a loom in Otavalo.

Symphonie in Blau auf einem Webstuhl in Otavalo.

La sal se obtiene por evaporación del agua marina.

Rien de bien nouveau, comme partout dans le monde, le sel s'obtient par l'évaporation des eaux de mer.

Salt extracted by the evaporation of sea water.

Hier wird nach althergebrachten Rezepten gearbeitet... das Salz erhält man durch Verdunsten des Meerwassers.

La misma refinería (todo parecido al centro cultural Georges Pompidou de París, es pura coincidencia).

La même raffinerie (toute ressemblance avec le centre culturel Georges Pompidou à Paris est purement accidentelle).

The same refinery (any resemblance to the Georges Pompidou Cultural Centre in Paris is purely coincidental).

Dieselbe Raffinerie, und es handelt sich hier nicht um das Kulturzentrum "Georges Pompidou" in Paris. Es ist ein reiner Zufall.

Refinería de Esmeraldas, un gran paso adelante.

Raffinerie de Esmeraldas, un grand pas en avant dans l'essor du pays.

The Esmeraldas refinery - a vast step forward in the development of the country.

Raffinerie in Esmeraldas, ein grosser Schritt vorwärts im Aufschwung des Landes.

Centro de control de una planta generadora de energía eléctrica.

Tableau de contrôle d'une centrale électrique.

Control panel of an electric power station.

Kontrollsaal eines Elektrizitätswerks.

← *Comunicaciones por satélite. El Ecuador marcha al ritmo de los tiempos.*

← *Communications par satellites. L'Equateur emboîte le pas du modernisme.*

← *Communication by satellites. Ecuador is stepping out on the road to modernization.*

← *Verbindung durch Satelitten. Ecuador schreitet mit dem Modernismus Hand in Hand.*

Final de pesca. Manta.

Retour de pêche. Manta.

Rückkehr vom Fischfang, Manta.

Return from fishing, Manta.

Pesca diaria para diario vivir.

Pêche quotidienne pour la vie de tous les jours.

Fishing, a ritual, daily act.

Fischfang... Rituelle und tägliche Geste.

Indios colorados - Viven en la zona occidental de la provincia de Pichincha.
Adornos corporales en base a un colorante llamado achiote. Los hombres convierten su cabello en casco con dicha planta.

Indiens "Colorados". Ils vivent dans la zone occidentale de la province de Pichincha. Peinture corporelle à base d'un colorant appelé "Achiote". A l'aide de cette plante les hommes transforment leur chevelure en casque.

"Colorado" Indians. They inhabit the western part of Pichincha Province. The body is painted with a colouring matter known as "Achiote". By means of this plant the men turn their hair into a hat.

"Colorado"-Indianer... Sie leben in der westlichen Zone der Provinz Pichincha.
Ein "Achiote" genannter Farbstoff. Die Männer benutzen diese Pflanze, um ihre Haare in einen "Helm" zu verwandeln.

Muchacha joven moliendo caña en un trapiche sui generis.
Jeune fille broyant la canne à sucre dans un moulin sui generis.
Girl crushing sugar cane in an improvised mill.
Junges Mädchen zermalmt Zuckerrohr in einer eigens dazu bestimmten Mühle.

Río y selva, Santo Domingo de los Colorados.

Rivière et forêt. Santo Domingo de los Colorados.

River and forest, Santo Domingo of Colorado.

Fluss und Wald... (Santo Domingo de los Colorados).

Artesano imaginero. Bordadora indígena. La destreza manual es común en el Ecuador.

Artisan imagier; brodeuse indigène. L'habileté manuelle est la chose du monde la mieux partagée en Equateur.

Image maker and embroiderer. Manual dexterity is the thing most fairly distributed in Ecuador.

Figurenselnitzer und eingeborene Stickerin. Geschicklichkeit und Erfindung sind charakteristisch für das ecuadorianische Kunstgewerbe.

En medio de la selva oriental del Ecuador vive el grupo de los Jivaros, cuya población no excede de los 5.000 habitantes. Cazadores y pescadores hábiles, tienen una enorme riqueza de rasgos culturales específicos. Conservan ceremonias rituales y técnicas esotéricas extrañas.

Desde épocas lejanas han venido practicando la reducción de las cabezas de sus enemigos - Tzantzas - por motivos rituales. Extraen los huesos del cráneo y someten la piel a una cocción de hierbas aborígenes, que reducen la cabeza a un tercio de su tamaño normal. La acción del humo termina este proceso reductor. Esta costumbre ritual, que los occidentales calificamos eróneamente de "salvaje", tiende a desaparecer. Efectivamente, en la actualidad los Jívaros hacen tzantzas de piel de cabra para engañar a los turistas.

Los Jívaros, así como otros grupos tribales del Oriente ecuatoriano, poseen mitos sobre su origen de gran riqueza imaginativa. Practican leyes de convivencia social y técnicas perfectamente adaptadas al medio ecológico en que viven.

Conocen las propiedades de hierbas curativas, tienen gran vitalidad como creadores de objetos estéticos, tales como tallas de madera, piezas cerámicas y adornos corporales llenos de color y vida.

El etnocentrismo que caracteriza a nuestra cultura occidental, nos lleva a hablar de "primitivismo" allí donde hay tan sólo diversidad cultural. Los grupos humanos predatores necesitan un amplio espacio geagráfico para procurarse proteínas y calorías. Toda reducción de su medio ambiente, de su habitat, conducirá fatalmente a su extinción como grupo socio-cultural.

Au cœur de la forêt orientale de l'Equateur vit la tribu des Jivaros qui n'excède pas 5.000 membres. Chasseurs et pêcheurs particulièrement habiles, ils possèdent un patrimoine culturel d'une richesse extraordinaire, pratiquant des cérémonies rituelles dont les techniques ésotériques sont étranges. Depuis la nuit des temps ils pratiquent la réduction des têtes de leurs ennemis (Tzantzas) pour des raisons rituelles.

Ils extraient les os du crâne et soumettent la peau à une décoction d'herbe aborigène qui réduit la tête à un tiers de sa taille. L'action de la fumée parachève le travail de réduction de cette espèce de tisane. Cette coutume rituelle que les occidentaux qualifient de "sauvage" tend à disparaître. En fait actuellement les Jivaros font des têtes réduites, qu'ils continuent d'appeler Tzantzas, du nom de leurs ennemis ancestraux, avec de la peau de chèvre. Ils trompent les touristes mais nous ne croyons pas que ceux-ci soient dupes.

Les Jivaros comme les autres tribus équatoriennes de l'est du pays, ont des rites et légendes riches en imagination.

Leurs lois sociales et leur manière de vivre sont parfaitement adaptées à leur milieu écologique. Nul ne connaît mieux que les Jivaros les vertus des plantes, nul n'a plus qu'eux de talent créateur dans le domaine de l'artisanat.

Connaissance des plantes quant à leur vertu curative, génie créateur dans le domaine de l'artisanat (travail du bois, de la céramique, des tissus destinés à l'habillement) voilà quelques qualités des Jivaros.

L'ethnocentrisme caractéristique de notre culture occidentale nous conduit à parler de "primitif" où existe seulement la diversité culturelle. Les groupes humains prédateurs nécessitent un vaste espace géographique pour se procurer protéines et calories. Toute réduction de leur milieu écologique conduisait fatalement à leur disparition en tant que groupe socio-culturel.

In the heart of the eastern forest of Ecuador lives the Jivaros tribe, whose number does not exceed 5,000. These highly skilled fishers and hunters have an extraordinarily abundant cultural heritage and practise certain ritual ceremonies, the esoteric techniques of which are somewhat strange. Since the dawn of time it has been their practice to shrink the heads of their enemies (Tzantzas) for reasons connected with their religion.

In order to do this, they first extract all the bone from the cranium. They then subject the remainder to a decoction of herbs which reduces the head to one third of its original size, after which it is smoked to complete the job. This ritual, which Westerners describe as "savage", is showing a tendency to disappear. Nowadays, the Jivaros continue to produce shrunken heads and still call them Tzantzas after the name of their ancestral enemies, but they make them from goatskin. These take in the tourists, but probably not the Jivaros themselves.

Like the other Ecuadorian tribes in the East of the country, the Jivaros have highly imaginative rites and legends.

Their customs and way of life are perfectly adapted to their ecological environment. No people are better acquainted with the virtues of plants than the Jivaros, and none has a greater creative talent in the field of craftsmanship (woodworking, pottery and clothing fabrics).

The characteristic self-centred attitude of our western culture leads us to describe as "primitive" that which is merely a different culture. Tribes living by hunting need vast geographical areas in order to procure proteins and calories, and any reduction of this environment would inevitably lead to their extinction as a socio-cultural group.

Im Herzen der im Osten von Ecuador gelegenen Wälder lebt der Stamm der Jivaros, der kaum 5.000 Menschen zählt. Diese sind besonders geschickte Jäger und Fischer; sie besitzen eine besonders reiche Kultur; sie üben rituelle Zeremonien aus, die mit seltsamen esoterischen Techniken verbunden sind. Seit uralten Zeiten reduzieren sie die Köpfe ihrer Feinde (Tzantzas) aus rituellen Gründen.

Sie entfernen die Schädelknochen und unterziehen die Haut einer Einwirkung von einem aus einheimischen Kräutern hergestellten Gebräu, das den Kopf auf ein Drittel seiner vorherigen Grösse reduziert. Die Einwirkung von Dampf vollendet die Reduzierungsarbeit dieses Gebräus. Diese rituelle Sitte, die die Bewohner der westlichen Hemisphäre als Gebräuche von Wilden bezeichnen, wird immer seltener ausgeführt. Auch heute noch stellen die Jivaros reduzierte Köpfe her, die sie auch weiterhin Tzantzas nennen (nach dem Namen ihrer Erbfeinde); aber diese Köpfe sind aus Ziegenhaut hergestellt. Nur wenige Touristen lassen sich dadurch täuschen.

Die Jivaros haben, wie auch die anderen ecuadorianischen Stämme im Osten des Landes, an Vorstellungskraft reiche Gebräuche und Sagen.

Ihre Sozialgesetze und ihre Lebensart sind ihrem ekologischen Milieu vollkommen angepasst. Niemand kennt besser als die Jivaros die Tugenden der Pflanzen und niemand übertrifft sie in der Ausübung der verschiedensten Kunstgewerbe.

Pflanzenkunde, besonders was ihre Heilkraft anbetrifft, ein schöpferisches Genie im Kunstgewerbe (Holzschnitzereien, Keramik, Kleiderstoffe), das sind einige Qualitäten der Jivaros.

Das charakteristische nur auf sich selbst Bezogensein unserer westlichen Kultur, treibt uns dazu, als primitiv zu bezeichnen, was nur kulturelle Verschiedenheit ist. Die von Jagd lebenden Stämme benötigen einen weiten geographischen Raum, um sich Protein und Kalorien zu verschaffen. Jedwede Reduzierung ihrer ökologischen Umwelt würde fatalerweise zu ihrem Verschwinden als sozial-kulturelle Gruppe führen.

El adorno del hombre es más abundante que el de la mujer. Usan plumas de tucán o Dios-te-dé. (Jívaros).

La parure de l'homme est plus abondante que celle de la femme; ils utilisent des plumes de Tucan ou Dios-te-Dé (Jivaros).

The adornment of the men is more abundant than that of the women; they use the feathers of the Toucan.

Die Männer sind schöner geschmückt als die Frauen. Sie benutzen Tukanfedern oder "Dios-te-Dé" (Jivaro).

Lanzas de chonta les sirven para las faenas de cacería. La chonta es una madera extremadamente dura y negra de la zona. Jívaros.

Des lances en Chonta sont utilisées pour la chasse. La chonta est un bois extrêmement dur et noir de la région des Jivaros.

Spears made of an extremely hard, black wood found in the Jivaros region and known as "chonta" are used for hunting.

Chonta-Lanzen werden für die Jagd verwendet. Das "Chonta" ist ein äusserst hartes schwarzes Holz aus dem Gebiet der Jivaros.

Pucuna, bodoquera o cerbatana, arma para cazar aves. Las flechas, envenenadas con curare, son lanzadas con extraordinaria precisión y fuerza.

Pucuna, bodequera ou sarbacane, arme pour chasser des oiseaux. Les flèches empoisonnées avec du curare sont lancées avec force et extrême précision.

The pucuna, bodequera or sarbacane, a weapon used for hunting birds. The arrows, poisoned with curare, are fired with force and extreme accuracy.

"Pucuna", "Bodequera" oder Blasrohr ist eine Waffe für Vogeljagd. Die mit "Curare" vergifteten Pfeile werden mit grosser Kraft und äusserster Genauigkeit abgeschossen.

Ceremonia ritual frente a la cascada.

Cérémonie rituelle, face à la cascade.

Ritual ceremony in front of the waterfall.

Rituelle Zeremonie vor einem Wasserfall.

...de lo humano y lo divino.

De l'humain au Divin.

From the human to the divine.

Vom Menschlichen zum Göttlichen.

Sangay : 5,323 m.

Orgullo de hombre.

Orgueil de l'Homme.

Human pride.

Menschlicher Stolz.

Placidez fluvial.

Calme sur le fleuve.

Calm on the river.

Ruhe auf dem Strom.

Ofrenda.

Offrande.

An offering.

Darbringung.

Muchacha jívara.

Jeune fille Jívara.

Jivaro girl.

Junges Jivaromädchen.

Grupo de Cofanes en el nororiente, zona del río Aguarico.

Groupe de Cofanes au Nord Est, région du fleuve Aguarico.

A group of Cofanes from the north-east in the region of the Aguarico River.

Cofanesgruppe im Nordosten, Gebiet des Stromes Aguarico.

Dos generaciones y el tiempo no ha pasado.

Deux générations, mais le temps ne passe pas.

Two generations, but time stands still.

Zwei Generationen in stehengebliebener Zeit.

Con el imperdible llega la aculturación.

Avec l'épingle de nourrice arrive l'acculturation.

Acculturation arrives with the safety pin.

Die Zivilisation erscheint mit der Sicherheitsnadel.

Flauta y tambores. Fiesta de Cofanes.

Flûte et tambours. Fête des Cofanes.

Flute and drums. The Cofanes feast day.

Flöte und Trommeln... ein Fest der Cofanes.

Diálogo.

Dialogue.

Dialog.

Cóndor: patrón de altura

Condor : maître des sommets

Condor, master of the heights

Der Kondor: der König der Gipfel

Paz en la altura.

Paix sur les hauteurs.

Peace in the uplands.

Friede auf den Höhen.

GALAPAGOS

El archipiélago Galápagos es un conjunto de trece islas y diez y siete islotes de orígen volcánico Presenta un interés excepcional para la ciencia, pues cada especie animal o vegetal ha sufrido un proceso de adaptación al medio ambiente que, a través de milenios, ha dado como resultado la presencia de especies vivas únicas en el planeta.

Cuando en 1835 Charles Darwin visita las islas de Galápagos y formula su teoría de la evolución de las especies, produce una conmoción en la sociedad tradicional y victoriana de Inglaterra y en toda la ciencia de la época. El hombre dá un paso adelante en la comprensión del mundo que le rodea.

Galápagos encierra una gran poesía de paisajes insólitos con su vegetación de cactus gigantes y arbustos blanquecinos que crecen sobre la lava, el granito y el basalto. En ese maravilloso mundo, se han producido dramas húmanos que son mezcla de leyenda y realidad, tal es el caso de la desaparición de la baronesa Héloïse Bosquet von Wagner y sus acompañantes Lorenz y Phillipson. Este suceso, de lo que ahora se ha dado en llamar realismo mágico, occurió en 1934.

Las cavernas naturales de lava en donde se refugiaban los piratas y flibusteros en el siglo XVII, son testimonio de un pasado apasionante poblado de tesoros escondidos, aventuras de balleneros y vidas de seres excéntricos que han buscado en Galápagos el perdido y nunca encontrado Edén.

Las focas de las islas, con sus gemidos que recuerdan el grito de mujer, nos hacen pensar en la vieja leyenda helénica de las sirenas. Las iguanas de tierra, con su terrible aspecto de monstruos prehístóricos, nos hablan de la era de los grandes reptiles y nos llevan, en un viaje fascinante, a través del tiempo hacia el remoto pasado de la gestación de la tierra.

Es reconfortante saber que este paraiso volcánico está actualmente protegido para la ciencia universal gracias a la acción del Gobierno ecuatoriano que ha delcarado Parque Nacional a las islas.

En Santa Cruz funciona la estación científica "Charles Darwin" que labora eficazmente para mantener un equilibrio ecológico que, con mayor fuerza cadadia, es una necesidad vital en este planeta que se va ensuciando y dañando por un insensato afán de lucro.

Viaje al pasado, a la leyenda y a la poesía; reencuentro con la naturaleza, baño reconfortante que nos devuelve la fé en el futuro del hombre, éso es Galápagos.

El paraíso está aquí. Galápagos.

Le Paradis est ici. Galapagos.

Galapagos. Here is Paradise.

Das Paradies auf Erden: die Galapagos Inseln.

No sólo de pan vive el hombre.

L'homme ne vit pas que de pain.

Man doth not live by bread alone.

Der Mensch lebt nicht von Brot allein.

A través de milénios. Iguanas de tierra.

Venus du fond des âges. Iguanes de terre.

From past ages; land iguanas.

Bild der Urzeit... Leguane.

Tortuga gigante o galápago (geochelone elephantopus).

Tortue géante ou galápago (geochelone elephantopus).

Giant tortoise or galapagos (geochelone elephantopus).

Riesenschildkröten oder Galapagos (Geochelone Elephantopus).

Siesta y vigía en las doradas arenas de Galápagos.

Sieste et malgré tout vigilance sur les sables dorés des Galapagos.

The siesta (with a watchful eye) on the golden sands of Galapagos.

In wachsamer Ruhe auf dem goldenen Sand der Galapagos.

Faenas marinas en Puerto Baquerizo, capital de la provincia de Galápagos.

Travaux à Puerto Baquerizo, capitale de la province de Galápagos.

Work in progress at Puerto Baquerino, capital of Galapagos Province.

Arbeiten in Puerto Baquerizo, der Hauptstadt der Provinz Galapagos.

Langostas sobre basalto.

Lobsters on basalt.

Langoustes sur basalte.

Langusten auf Basaltgestein.

The Galapagos Archipelago consists of thirteen large and 17 small islands of volcanic origin. It is of exceptional interest for scientists, since each animal and plant species has undergone a process of adaptation to the environment; this process, which has gone on for thousands of years has resulted in a presence of species which are unique in the world.

When Charles Darwin visited the Galapagos Archipelago in 1835 and brought out his theory of the evolution of species, it produced a shock throughout the traditionalist society of Victorian England and among contemporary scientists.

Man made considerable progress in the understanding of his environment. Giant cactuses and trees from another world growing out of the lava, granite and basalt make Galapagos an unusual place in which even poetry is not lacking.

In this wonderful place occur human dramas in which legends are interwoven with reality - such as the disappearance of the Baroness Heloise Bosquet von Wagner and his companions Lorenz and Phillipson. This happened in 1934 and has an air of magic about it.

The caves of lava which were the refuge of the seventeenth century pirates and filibusters are evidence of a past which was particularly rich in hidden treasures, adventures of whalers and ecentric individuals who came to Galapagos to look for Paradise Lost, but never found it.

L'Archipel des Galapagos, comprend 13 îles et 17 îlots d'origine volcanique. Il présente un intérêt exceptionnel pour la science, car chaque espèce animale ou végétale a subi un processus d'adaptation au milieu ambiant qui, à travers des millénaires a eu comme résultat la présence d'espèces uniques sur la planète.

Quand, en 1835 Charles Darwin visita les Iles Galapagos et donna sa théorie sur l'évolution des espèces, il se produisit un choc dans la Société traditionnelle et victorienne d'Angleterre et dans toute la science de l'époque.

L'homme fit un progrès considérable dans la compréhension de son environnement. Cactus géants et arbres d'un autre monde poussant sur la lave. Le granit et le basalte donnent aux Galapagos, un univers insolite qui ne manque pas de poésie.

Dans ce merveilleux endroit du monde, se produisent des drames humains où s'entrecroisent légendes et réalités telle que la disparition de la baronne Heloïse Bosquet von Wagner et ses compagnons Lorenz et Phillipson - ceci se produisit en 1934 et relève de la magie.

Les cavernes de laves où se sont réfugiés les pirates et les flibustiers au XVIIème siècle sont le témoignage d'un passé particulièrement riche de trésors cachés, d'aventures de chasseurs de baleines, et des vies d'êtres excentriques qui cherchèrent aux Galapagos le Paradis perdu et jamais retrouvé.

Les phoques de ces îles avec leurs gémissements qui ressemblent au cri de la femme, nous rappellent la vieille légende hellénique des sirènes.

Les iguanes, avec leur aspect de monstres préhistoriques nous retracent l'ère des grands reptiles et nous transportent, par un voyage fascinant à travers le temps, dans le lointain passé de la terre en gestation.

Il est réconfortant de savoir que ce paradis volcanique est actuellement protégé pour la science universelle ceci grâce à l'action du gouvernement équatorien qui a déclaré les îles Parc National.

A Santa Cruz, fonctionne un centre de recherches scientifiques "Charles Darwin" qui travaille efficacement pour maintenir un équilibre écologique.

Cet équilibre apparait, chaque jour avec plus de force, comme une nécessité vitale pour cette planète polluée et défigurée par la recherche insensée du profit. Voyage dans le passé, les légendes et la poésie, contact avec la nature, réconfort qui nous redonne la foi dans l'avenir de l'homme.

Voilà les Galapagos !

The seals in these islands, with their cry like that of a woman, remind us of the Greek legend about sirens.

The iguanas, looking like prehistoric monsters, bring back to us the era of the great reptiles and take us on a fascinating journey through time to the remote past days of the gestation of the earth.

It is comforting to know that this volcanic paradise is now protected for international science thanks to the action of the Ecuadorian Government, which has declared the islands a national park.

In Santa Cruz there is a "Charles Darwin" Scientific Research Centre, which is doing useful work in keeping the ecological balance.

This is a function the importance of which is mounting every day on this planet, which is increasingly polluting and degrading itself due to an insensate longing for profit.

A journey, then, into the past, legends and poetry, and a contact with nature which restore our faith in the future of the human being.

That is Galapagos.

Der Archipel der Galapagos umfasst 13 Inseln und siebzehn Inselchen vulkanischen Ursprungs. Er ist für die Wissenschaft von ausserordentlichem Interesse, denn jede Tier- oder Pflanzengattung wurde einem Angleichungsprozess unterworfen, der es ihnen ermöglichte, in dem sie umgebenden Milieu Fuss zu fassen. Das Resultat war, dass im Laufe der Jahrtausende hier auf der Erde einzigartige Wesen erhalten blieben.

Als Charles Darwin im Jahre 1835 die Galapagos-Inseln besuchte und daraufhin seine Theorie über die Entwicklung der Arten entstand, wurde das ein Schock für die traditionelle, viktorianische Gesellschaft Englands und für die ganze damalige Wissenschaft.

Die Menschen erhielten so immer grösseres Verständnis für ihre Umgebungswelt. Riesenkakteen und Bäume aus einer anderen Welt, die auf Lavaboden wuchsen. Granit und Basalt geben den Galapagos-Inseln ein ungewöhnliches Aussehen, das voller Poesie ist.

In diesem wundervollen Ort fanden menschliche Dramen statt, in denen sich Legende und Wirklichkeit kreutzen, wie das Verschwinden der Baronin Heloise Bosquet von Wagners und seiner Begleiter Lorenz und Phillipson - Das, was im Jahre 1934 stattfand, kann man nur der Zauberei zuschreiben.

Die Lavagrotten, die Piraten und Freibeutern im XVII. Jahrhundert Unterschlupf boten, legen Zeugnis ab von einer Vergangenheit reich an verborgenen Schätzen, wo auch die Walfischjäger eine Rolle spielten. Hier lebten auch exzentrische Menschen, die auf den Galapagos-Inseln, das verlorene und nie wiedergefundene Paradies suchten.

Die Seehunde dieser Inseln, deren Winseln Frauenschreien ähnelt, erinnern uns an die alte griechische Sage von den Sirenen.

Die Rieseneidechsen, die vorsinnflutlichen Ungeheuern ähneln, rufen in uns die Erinnerung an die grossen Reptilien wach und versetzen uns in einer faszinierenden Reise in alte Zeiten zurück.

Es ist äusserst beruhigend festzustellen, dass dieses Vulkanparadies jetzt von der universellen Wissenschaft geschützt wird, und das dank des Eingreifens der ecuadorianischen Regierung, die diese Inseln zum Nationalpark erklärte.

In Santa Cruz funktioniert das Institut "Charles Darwin", das sich mit wissenschaftlichen Untersuchungen befasst; es arbeitet in wirksamer Weise an der Einhaltung eines ekologischen Gleichgewichts.

Dieses Gleichgewicht setzt sich jeden Tag mit grösserer Dringlichkeit als vitale Notwendigkeit für unsere so schwer unter Umweltverschmutzung leidende Welt durch, die ebenfalls durch wahnwitzige Profitgier verunstaltet wird.

Paisaje selenita con pájaros. Islas Galápagos.

Moonscape with birds. The Galapagos Islands.

Paysage lunaire avec oiseaux. Iles Galapagos.

"Mondlandschaft" mit Vögeln. Die Galapagos-Inseln

Comunión ecológica de troncos y flamingos.

Harmonie écologique entre les troncs d'arbres et les flamants.

Ecological harmony between the tree trunks and the flamingoes.

Ekologische Harmonie zwischen Bäumen und Flamingos.

Pájaro, basalto y mar. Islas Galápagos.

Oiseau, basalte et mer. Iles Galapagos.

Bird, basalt and the sea. Galapagos Islands.

▼ *Vogel, Basalt und Meer. Galapagos-Inseln.*

Cet ouvrage a été imprimé sur les Presses
des Editions DELROISSE
113, rue de Paris - 92100 BOULOGNE - France

Photogravure : Fotomecanica Iberico - MADRID
Photos : BODO WUTH - Mlle MOREL -
Dominique DELAVERGNE - Jean-Claude KOSTER

Textes : M. Juan CUEVA Jaramillo -
Conseiller Culturel à l'Ambassade de l'Equateur
auprès de la République Française

Dépôt légal N° 772
ISBN 2-85518-018-X